W9-BMG-890

Macbeth
A Resource Book

Amsco books by Joan D. Berbrich

Fifteen Steps to Better Writing
Laugh Your Way Through Grammar
Macbeth: A Resource Book
101 Ways to Learn Vocabulary
Reading Around the World
Reading Today
Thirteen Steps to Better Writing
Wide World of Words
Writing About Amusing Things
Writing About Curious Things
Writing About Fascinating Things
Writing About People
Writing Creatively
Writing Logically
Writing Practically

Macbeth
A Resource Book

Joan D. Berbrich, Ph.D.

When ordering this book, please specify either
R 484 W *or* MACBETH: A RESOURCE BOOK

Dedicated to serving
AMSCO
our nation's youth

FRANKLIN PIERCE
COLLEGE LIBRARY
RINDGE, N.H. 03461

Amsco School Publications, Inc.
315 Hudson Street / New York, N.Y. 10013

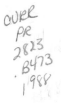

CURR
PR
2823
. B473
1988

ISBN 0-87720-779-8

Copyright © 1988 by Amsco School Publications, Inc.
No part of this book may be reproduced in any form
without written permission from the publisher.
Printed in the United States of America

Preface

A comet flashes across the sky, startles us with its brilliance, and—is gone. In the world of arts there are many comets: playwrights and actors and artists and musicians who are popular today, even adored, and tomorrow forgotten.

A few—like Hemingway, and Gershwin, and Klee—last longer: fifty years, even a hundred. But then they seem to acquire a patina of moss and survive only as nostalgic reminders of an earlier age.

And a very few, like bright stars, remain forever. Think of Michelangelo and Leonardo, think of Dante and Beethoven. Think of Shakespeare.

To his peers, to the people who lived in his own time, Shakespeare must have seemed a rather ordinary man. He had a moderately successful marriage; he had three children; he acquired a modest fortune. He was a pretty good actor, a respected director, a fairly astute businessman.

But in one way he was not ordinary, but extraordinary . . . as a playwright.

He dug into history for characters and incidents that illumined his age and ours.

He probed into the minds of his created people to discover, and express, truths more far-reaching, more valid, than the truths proclaimed by some psychiatrists.

He clustered words into sentences; he coined words when his impatient brain could not find satisfactory ones; he made our language richer, sharper, more piquant.

This ordinary man . . . this extraordinary playwright . . . this William Shakespeare.

In this volume we are concerned with only one of his plays: *Macbeth*. It is a short play, a readable play, a play which has at least as much to say to us today as it had to his peers in the seventeenth century. It is, at the same time, a typical play. Consider *Macbeth* a model, a prototype. When you have finished a careful reading of *Macbeth,* you will be ready to read any Shakespearean play; for the foundation will have been built.

Why do you need a resource guide to read *Macbeth*? Why should you spend time on a book of this type? Why can't you just pick up *Macbeth* and read it?

Well, you can, of course. But four centuries DO make a difference, and our background is often inadequate. As you read, questions shoot to the surface. If you pause to find the answers, you break the continuity of your reading and lessen the impact of the play. Besides, you would have to consult dozens of books to find all the answers. Would you?

> You can use this book in class, with group discussions and teacher-led analysis. Or you can use it by yourself. Either way, it can be a kind of private tutor, posing questions and guiding you to appropriate answers.

So, in this one slim volume, the questions have been collected—and answered. Questions like these:

Is *Macbeth* based on actual historical incidents? Was there really a conflict between Macbeth and King Duncan? What is a thane? Did Shakespeare write this play for King James? Why? (See Unit I.)

Did Shakespeare coin words? Did he enrich our language? Have some words changed in meaning since his time? What phrases did he create that live today? (See Unit II.)

What was Shakespeare's theater like? Was the stage different from the modern stage? How did this affect the development of certain techniques? What is equivocation? Why did Shakespeare refer to it? Is it still used today? How did Shakespeare use current events to make his plays vital and meaningful to his audience? (See Unit III.)

When and why did Shakespeare use alliteration? Rhymed couplets? Iambic pentameter? Allusions? Similes? Imagery? How did the minimal use of setting and props influence his writing? (See Unit IV.)

What are the characteristics of a tragedy? How did Shakespeare make his characters seem real and alive? How did he handle dialogue? Why was dialogue more important then than it is today? What is foreshadowing? When did Shakespeare use it? (See Unit V.)

What can an analysis of just a few scenes teach us about Shakespeare's writing? How did he make all the above elements (Units I through V) work together? What is a soliloquy? Why did Shakespeare use soliloquies? (See Unit VI.)

All the answers to the above questions are important. They give us insight into Macbeth's time, into Shakespeare's age, into our own era.

Yet the biggest question of all remains unanswered: why read Shakespeare at all? If reading his plays properly takes work, why bother? Why not just read the plays of Tennessee Williams, or Kaufman and Hart, or Ken Kesey?

The answer is astonishingly simple because Shakespeare, somehow, makes a direct piercing appeal to most of us. Again, consider *Macbeth*.

To write it, Shakespeare took history and twisted it to fit his story. Obviously he wasn't interested in writing a simple history play. He wanted, instead, to depict a certain kind of man—a man overwhelmed by a desire for power, darkened by hubristic ambition. He wanted to show us a man who rationalized his evil deeds, who used his wife, and superstition, and history itself to justify his actions. And in doing so, Shakespeare forces each one of us to recall the many times we too have sought sham reasons for wrongful acts.

What is the secret of Shakespeare's magic? I don't know. Master the information in this book; study his techniques; analyze his use of sources. And, of course, read the play. Then perhaps *you* will know.

And if you don't, it makes little difference. The magic is there; and it is now yours.

Contents

UNIT I   **BACKGROUND**

1. What?   1
2. Where?   1
3. When?   4
4. Why?   6
5. Who?   8
6. Source?   10

UNIT II   **WORDS, WORDS, WORDS**

7. Elizabethan Word Bank, Part I   13
8. Elizabethan Word Bank, Part II   15
9. Animal Lore   19
10. Military Words   22
11. Words That Have Changed Their Meanings   26
12. Shakespeare's Language Legacy   29

UNIT III   **STAGE AND HISTORY**

13. Shakespeare's Stage   34
14. Equivocation   38
15. The "News" in *Macbeth*   40
16. The Order of the Universe   45

UNIT IV   WRITING TECHNIQUES

17.   Alliteration   48
18.   Rhymed Couplets   49
19.   Verse   51
20.   Allusions   53
21.   Similes   59
22.   Imagery   61

UNIT V   STRUCTURE

23.   Structure   65
24.   Characterization   69
25.   Dialog   73
26.   Foreshadowing   77

UNIT VI   ANALYSIS OF KEY SCENES

27.   The Witches' Prophecies   81
28.   The Witches' Prophecies (continued)   82
29.   The Witches' Prophecies (continued)   85
30.   A Dagger of the Mind?   87
31.   A Barren Scepter   90
32.   Tomorrow, and Tomorrow, and Tomorrow   92

Background

1. What?

MACBETH, a play by William Shakespeare.

About . . . Macbeth,
    a general in the King's army, a valiant fighter
but also . . .
    a man who dreamed of becoming a king.
To win the crown, he murdered.
To keep the crown, he murdered . . . and murdered once more,
    and murdered yet again.

The story includes the slaughter of children, a beheading, horses that eat horses, and trees that walk. Witches open the play, and ghosts with "gory locks" appear at will. Battles rage—and betrayal—and treason. It is the most melodramatic of all melodramas, a bath in blood, a drowning in violence.

How could such a play hold millions of spectators in rapt and awed attention for some 400 years?

Perhaps we see Macbeth, even today, in many of our world leaders—both the slain and the slayers. Perhaps we see Macbeth in some of our business executives who, caught up in the race for success, trample on the humanity of others—and on their own. Perhaps we see a little of Macbeth in ourselves . . . and we respond with fear and self-doubt.

Whatever the cause, *Macbeth* lives—a monument to the mixture of good and evil in all of us.

2. Where?

In SCOTLAND:

FORRES: the site of Duncan's palace
INVERNESS: Macbeth's castle
FIFE: Macduff's castle
SCONE: where Kings of Scotland were crowned

Macbeth's Scotland

(Note: A *Firth* is a long, narrow inlet of a sea.)

DUNSINANE: where Macbeth takes up residence late in the play
BIRNAM WOOD: near Dunsinane

Also, the heath, the desert, and a cavern . . . and briefly . . .

In ENGLAND:

The King's Palace (Edward the Confessor)

Answer the following questions, using the map to help you find the answers.

1. In a camp near *Forres,* King Duncan and his sons receive a report from the battlefield. (Act I, Scene ii, lines 54–60) In what part of Scotland is *Forres* located?

   _____

2. DUNCAN: Whence cam'st thou, worthy thane?
   ROSS: From Fife, great king;
        Where the Norweyan banners flout the sky
        And fan our people cold. Norway himself
        With terrible numbers,
        Assisted by that most disloyal traitor
        The thane of Cawdor, began a dismal conflict . . .

   a. Where did the main battle take place? Describe briefly its location.

   _____

   _____

   b. The Norweyans (Norwegians) apparently invaded Scotland to help the rebels. Where did they probably land?

   _____

   c. The thane of Cawdor turns out to be a traitor. In what part of Scotland was his home (Cawdor) located?

   _____

3. Macbeth and Banquo arrive at Forres. About how far did they travel from the battlefield? (Use the scale of miles on the map.)

   _____

4. Soon Duncan announces he will meet Macbeth at Macbeth's castle in Inverness. Where in Scotland is Inverness located?

   _____

5. MACDUFF: He [Macbeth] is already named, and gone to Scone
        To be invested.
        ("To be invested" means "to be crowned.")
   Where in Scotland is Scone located?

   _____

6.   Macbeth shall never vanquish'd be until
                      Great Birnam wood to high Dunsinane hill
                      Shall come against him.

   a. Near the end of the play, Macbeth and Lady Macbeth are in residence at Dunsinane. Where in Scotland is Dunsinane located?

   _____

b. Where is Birnam wood located?

_____

c. Why do you suppose Macbeth feels very sure of himself after he hears this prediction?

_____

_____

3. When?

In 1034, Duncan became King, founding the first and only dynasty of Scotland. The action in the play, *Macbeth,* began six years later, in 1040. At that time Duncan was 36 years old, although Shakespeare depicts him as an old man.

Scotland, in Duncan's time, was still unsettled. It had taken the name "Scotland" only 200 years earlier, and it was still the site of frequent battles as various chieftains fought for power.

What do we know about Scotland at that time?

FEUDALISM: Scotland was a feudal society in 1040 (11th century). This means the thanes (lords) were very powerful, and all other people were ruled by them. The king was not really supreme—merely the first among equals. The result was that rebellion was common as one thane or another strove to become king.

CLANS: Clans (tribes) were the key to Scottish life. Loyalty was to one's clan and clan leader rather than to country and to king.

BLOOD FEUDS: Blood feuds raged, primarily between clans. Lady Macbeth was from a clan that had long been involved in a blood feud with Duncan's clan.

HOSPITALITY: Hospitality was revered, as it was in most ancient and medieval societies. After all, there were few hotels and inns, and travelers depended on strangers for food and shelter. Each host, aware that he might be a traveler the next day or month, provided not only food and shelter but also protection.

VIOLENCE: It was a dangerous time to be a king. Seventeen kings ruled Scotland from 844 to 1057. Of these, twelve were assassinated.

DAILY LIFE: Life itself was a struggle. Food and water were scarce, especially for the common people. The strength of the Scots was spent in fighting each other and the Vikings.

VIKINGS: The Vikings (from Scandinavia) had ruled sections of Scotland for several centuries and the invading Norwegians may have been trying to bolster Viking domination.

FREEDOM: Freedom barely existed but it was eagerly sought. Said Ranulf Higden, a 14th century Briton: The Scots "be light of heart, strong and wild enough . . . They be cruel upon their enemies, and hate bondage most of anything, and hold it foul sloth if any man dieth in bed, and great worship if he die in the field."

Answer the following questions using the information you have just read.

1. In what year did King Duncan die? _____

2. Macbeth: He's (Duncan) here in double trust:
     First, as I am his kinsman and his subject,
     Strong both against the deed; then, as his host,
     Who should against his murderer shut the door,
     Not bear the knife myself.

   a. What does Macbeth seem to be planning to do?

   _____

   _____

   b. What custom of 11th-century Scottish society would Macbeth be breaking if he followed through with his plan?

   _____

   _____

3. Why was it natural (considering Scotland in the 11th century) for Lady Macbeth to urge her husband to do away with King Duncan?

   _____

   _____

4. In Act I, Scene ii, lines 18–25, a sergeant brings a report from the battlefield to Duncan:

                   For brave Macbeth—well he deserves that name—
                   Disdaining fortune, with his brandish'd steel
                   Which smok'd with bloody execution,
                   Like valor's minion carv'd out his passage
                   Till he fac'd the slave;
                   Which ne'er shook hands, nor bade farewell to him,
                   Till he unseam'd him from the nave to the chaps,
                   And fix'd his head upon our battlements.

   Read the above passage carefully. Remember it was spoken by a sergeant reporting to a king known to be gentle. What aspect of life in 11th-century Scotland is clearly depicted?

   _____

   _____

5. Siward, the English general, is told that his young son was just killed on the battlefield. "Had he his hurts before?" he asks, and Ross replies: "Aye, on the front." Without pause, Siward comments:

                        Why then, God's soldier be he!
                   Had I as many sons as I have hairs,
                   I would not wish them to a fairer death.

5

What aspect of life in 11th-century Scotland (and England) undoubtedly influenced Siward's reaction? Young Siward must have been just a couple of years older than you. What is your reaction to the father's words?

_____

_____

_____

4. Why?

Shakespeare wrote 37 plays. Only one was set in Scotland—*Macbeth.*

Shakespeare seemed to be in a hurry in 1606 when he wrote *Macbeth,* his shortest tragedy.

Why? The answer lies in another question: *Why* did Shakespeare write *Macbeth?*

Queen Elizabeth I died in 1603, leaving no children. The nearest relative, the heir to the throne, was James VI, King of Scotland. So James VI of Scotland became James I of England.

James was an odd fellow—rather stout and not too bright—against tobacco and fascinated by witches. In fact, James was so fervent a believer in witchcraft that, while he was King of Scotland, he spent much time ferreting out old women and torturing them until they confessed that they were, indeed, witches. One even admitted that she had gone to sea in a sieve to wreck a ship (possibly the one carrying James's wife-to-be) from Denmark!

In 1606 James was eagerly anticipating a visit from his brother-in-law, King Christian of Denmark. All sorts of parties and ceremonials were planned for the royal meeting. And, of course, James wanted a play—a new play written just for the occasion. Who better to write the play than the foremost playwright of the time—William Shakespeare?

With little doubt, Shakespeare wrote *Macbeth* with the royal celebrations in mind . . . and to flatter the new monarch. Consider the following features in *Macbeth:*

James was from Scotland. The new play would be set in Scotland.

James was a descendant of Banquo and indirectly of Duncan. The new play would depict Duncan and Banquo in favorable fashion.

James believed in witchcraft. The new play would start with three witches huddled over a cauldron—continue with the witches concocting prophecies for Macbeth—and follow through to the witches conjuring up apparitions (ghostly visions) that foretell the ending of the tale.

James believed in ghosts. The new play would have a ghost with gory locks sitting at a table.

James was proud of his ancestry. The new play would show Banquo's heirs (apparition-style)—eight of them—a long glorious line. And James, of course, would be the last!

And so *Macbeth* was presented before the royal pair—and we can be sure that James enjoyed every minute of it!

After reading the information on page 6, answer the following questions.

1. Was James I married? How do you know? _____

_____

2. What monarch (king or queen) did James I follow? _____

3. How many plays did Shakespeare write? _____

4. Who (according to Shakespeare) was the eighth king descended from Banquo? _____

_____

5. How did the authorities persuade old women to admit they were witches? _____

_____

6. A *sieve* is a device with small holes through which fine particles of sand (or other sub-
stances) will pass, separating them from coarser particles. Now read these four lines
spoken by the First Witch in *Macbeth* when a sailor's wife defies her.

> Her husband's to Aleppo gone, master o' the Tiger;
> But in a sieve I'll thither sail,
> And, like a rat without a tail,
> I'll do, I'll do, and I'll do.

a. Can you guess what the First Witch was planning to do?

_____

_____

b. What does her setting sail *in a sieve* tell us about her?

_____

_____

c. How does this passage reflect the interests of James I?

_____

_____

7. Which is the shortest tragedy Shakespeare wrote? _____

8. Why did Shakespeare probably write *Macbeth?* _____

_____

_____

9. Following is a brief (and incomplete) character sketch of James I. Using the information on page 6, complete the sketch by providing substantiating details.

James I of England was a complex character. He was superstitious.

_____

_____

_____

He was hospitable. _____

_____

_____

He was proud of his ancestry. _____

_____

_____

Above all, he enjoyed flattery. _____

_____

_____

10. Review rapidly all you already know about the play, *Macbeth*. Now list below as many features as you can that suggest that this play would be a "natural" for a television production.

_____

_____

_____

_____

_____

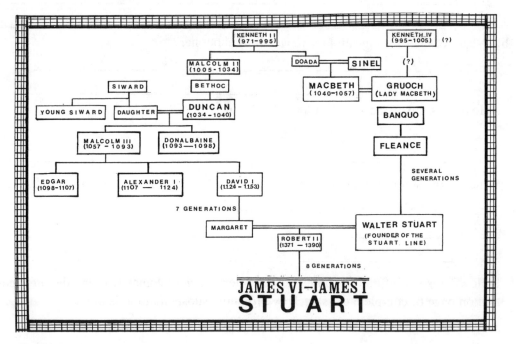

5. Who?

Here is a "family tree." For the moment, just glance over it, noting four names: DUNCAN, MACBETH, BANQUO, and JAMES I.

Now—as you read this text, check the names constantly with those on the chart.

Kenneth II and Kenneth IV were two kings, each from a specific clan. Kenneth II had two children: a boy, Malcolm, and a girl, Doada.

Malcolm, the son, became King Malcolm II and had a son, Bethoc, who apparently never ruled. But Malcolm's grandson, DUNCAN, was crowned after this grandfather's death.

Siward was an English general. His daughter (name unknown) married Duncan, so Siward was a natural ally of Duncan and his sons.

Duncan had two sons: Malcolm and Donalbain. The elder son became King Malcolm III after Macbeth's death.

Malcolm III had three sons. The youngest, David, had a descendant, Margaret.

Now we return for the moment to the top of the chart. (Keep checking constantly with the chart.)

Kenneth II's daughter, Doada, married the thane of Glamis, Sinel. They had one son, Macbeth, who became thane of Glamis when Sinel died.

Kenneth IV had a granddaughter, Gruoch, whom Macbeth married. (Notice that Macbeth is the grandson of Kenneth II and the grandson, through marriage, of Kenneth IV.) Macbeth and Lady Macbeth had no children.

Banquo may be a legendary figure, dreamed up to be the founder of the Stuart line. Banquo had one son, Fleance and a grandson, or great-grandson, Walter Stuart.

Now the two lines come together again.

Margaret (descendant of Kenneth II, Duncan, and Malcolm III) married Walter Stuart. From this marriage came a line of kings starting with Robert II and continuing on to James I.

If we were to continue the chart, we would discover that the present Queen of Great Britain, Elizabeth II, is a twelfth-generation descendant of King James I.

For the most part, this "family tree" provides the cast of characters for *Macbeth:*

> King Duncan and his sons, Malcolm and Donalbain
> Macbeth (a general) and Lady Macbeth
> Banquo (a general) and his son, Fleance
> Siward (English general) and his son, Siward

In addition:

> Macduff, Lady Macduff, and their children
> Ross, Lennox, Angus, and others (noblemen)
> + assorted minor characters

Consult the chart as needed to answer the following questions.

1. How many sons did Duncan have? Which was first in line for the throne?

_____

2. Who was Macbeth's father? Mother?

_____

3. Who is Fleance? What relationship does he have to James I?

_____

4. On what basis could Macbeth insist he was a legitimate contender for the crown of Scotland?

_____

_____

5. How was the English general Siward related to Duncan?

_____

_____

6. Early in the play, Duncan greets Macbeth as "O worthiest cousin!" Is he just being polite, or are the two men really cousins? If they are, *how* are they?

_____

_____

7. After Duncan's death, Macbeth says to Malcolm and Donalbain:

>The spring, the head, the fountain of your blood
>Is stopped; the very source of it is stopped.

What does Macbeth mean?

_____

_____

8. While collecting an army, Malcolm says:

>   gracious England hath
>Lent us good Siward and ten thousand men;
>An older and a better soldier none
>That Christendom gives out.

How else might Malcolm logically have talked of Siward?

_____

_____

6. Source?

Where did Shakespeare get his plots? Where did he find the historical information used in many of his plays?

For *Macbeth,* the answer is easy. Shakespeare found both plot and history in Holinshed's *Chronicles of England, Scotland, and Ireland,* published in 1577. But he used "poetic license" in handling this material. When it suited him, Shakespeare telescoped time, manipulated characters, and even combined two totally separate stories!

For example:

In Shakespeare's play, Duncan is an old, rather tired man, in contrast to Macbeth who is young and forceful. In actuality, in 1040, Duncan was 36 years old and Macbeth at least a few years older.

In Shakespeare's play, Macbeth murders Duncan while Duncan is asleep. In actuality, Macbeth met Duncan on the battlefield, fought with him, and killed him.

In Shakespeare's play, Lady Macbeth urges her husband to kill the king. In actuality, Lady Macbeth played no part in the king's death.

What Shakespeare did: he took the *fact*—that Macbeth slew Duncan—from Holinshed. But this wasn't strong enough, not sinister enough. So, also in Holinshed, he found another tale: of Donwald who murdered King Duff, and of Donwald's wife who urged that the deed be done. Shakespeare combined the two stories to develop his own plot for his own purposes.

In Shakespeare's play, Macbeth rules for only a short time. In actuality, Macbeth ruled for seventeen years and was considered a strong and kindly king.

Why did Shakespeare change history so radically? The answer seems obvious: to write a play that would please and flatter James I. James must have been delighted—first, because the new play proclaimed the sacred nature of a king and the duty to protect him; and second, because the new play built up *his* ancestors and strengthened his claim to the throne.

But Shakespeare had another reason for changing history. He wanted to write a play that would be a vehicle for one of his own deepest beliefs: that order in the universe is essential, and that human actions, distorted, can distort this order.

In the early 17th century, England was surrounded by enemies. It was vital that there be no civil war, no rebellion, no king-killing to confuse and divide the people. In *Macbeth*, Shakespeare examines the brutal killing of a king and proves that all of nature is affected by the deed. He was appalled; and we, reading or watching the play, are equally appalled.

Use the above information to answer the following questions.

1. Who wrote *Chronicles of England, Scotland, and Ireland?* In what year?

_____

2. Consider the phrase "poetic license" in paragraph 2. What does poetic license mean?

_____

_____

3.　　　　　　HOLINSHED: Duncan was killed on the battlefield.
　　　　　　SHAKESPEARE: Duncan was killed in bed.

Does the method of the killing make a difference in our attitude toward Duncan? Toward Macbeth? Explain your answers briefly.

_____

_____

FOR DISCUSSION

4. Have you ever seen a movie or a TV mini-series about one of our country's leaders—Washington or FDR, Martin Luther King, Jr., or Susan B. Anthony? How was the subject handled? Were any liberties taken with history? Is your present opinion of this person a direct result of the movie or TV program?

5. Evaluate Shakespeare's action in changing history to suit his needs. Consider these points:

   a. Was anyone hurt by the changes?
   b. Was anyone helped by the changes?
   c. Is it ever moral to change historical data?
   d. What dangers can result if history can be changed at whim?
   e. Does a writer of fiction and a writer of history have the same duty toward historical truth?

   After you have discussed these questions (and their answers), think . . . draw a conclusion . . . and write the results of your evaluation below.

   _____

   _____

   _____

   _____

   _____

   _____

UNIT II

Words, Words, Words

7. Elizabethan Word Bank—Part I

In England today you will hear unfamiliar words for familiar things: an elevator is a "lift" and gasoline is "petrol." You will also hear familiar words with unfamiliar meanings: a "chemist's" is a drugstore.

The same is true of language in Elizabethan times. Here are some words (both familiar and unfamiliar) that Shakespeare used in the play, *Macbeth*.

WEIRD: having to do with fate or destiny; the witches are "weird" because they foresee (and possibly influence) the future or destiny of humans.

POSTERS: a noun meaning "swift riders" (on horseback, or foot—or broomstick!)

POST: a messenger or "letter carrier" who, using fast horses, delivered mail rapidly. (A letter written by Essex left Plymouth on October 26, 1597 at 10:00 A.M. and arrived at Basingstoke the next day at 3:30 P.M., a distance of 165 miles in under thirty hours!)

HAUTBOYS: from the French *haut* meaning "high" and *bois* meaning "wood." Apparently used to name the present "oboe" because the oboe is a *wooden* instrument with a *high* pitch. The pronunciation of "oboe" is a corruption of the French.

OFFICES: servants' quarters

GROOMS: servants who slept at the foot of the king's bed

POSSET: warm drink of milk and ale, often taken just before retiring

SUBORNED: bribed

INVESTED: crowned

INSANE ROOT: henbane or hemlock, said to cause madness

SEWER: a server; a household official in charge of serving food (pronounced just like the word "sewer" meaning "a drain")

HUSBANDRY: thrift, economy

LARGESSE: gift of money

SURFEITED: overfed

CHARGE: the person (i.e. the king) for whom the grooms are responsible

PARLEY: conference of war

NAMED: elected

BENISON: blessing

Paraphrase (rewrite in your own words) the following quotations from *Macbeth* in order to show the meaning clearly. Use the Word Bank vocabulary to help you. The first two quotations are paraphrased for you as examples.

1.
> The doors are open, and the surfeited grooms
> Do mock their charge with snores. I have drugged their possets,
> That death and nature do contend about them,
> Whether they live or die. (Lady Macbeth to Macbeth about
> King Duncan and his grooms: II, ii, 5–9)

Paraphrase: The doors are open, and the servants, who have had too much to eat and drink, make fun of the person they're in charge of by sleeping. Lady Macbeth has drugged their evening drinks of warm milk and ale so that death and sleep are confused and it's hard to tell whether they're alive or dead.

2.
> What's the business,
> That such a hideous trumpet calls to parley
> The sleepers of a house? (Lady Macbeth when they find
> King Duncan dead: II, iii, 89–91)

Paraphrase: What kind of business is it that has a revolting trumpet wake the people who are sleeping and call them to a conference of war?

3.
> The weird sisters, hand in hand,
> Posters of the sea and land,
> Thus do go about, about. (I, iii, 32–34)

_____

_____

_____

4.
> As thick as hail
> Came post with post, and everyone did hear
> Thy praises . . .
> (spoken by Ross to Macbeth: I, iii, 99–101)

_____

_____

5.
> Were such things here as we do speak about?
> Or have we eaten on the insane root
> That takes the reason prisoner?
> (Banquo when the witches vanish: I, iii, 84–86)

_____

_____

6.   [Hautboys and torches. Enter the sewer, and divers servants
      with dishes and service . . .]
      (Stage direction: I, vii)

_____

_____

7.   There's husbandry in heaven,
      Their candles are all out. (Banquo to his son as they set
      out at night: II, i, 5–6)

_____

_____

8.   The King's abed.
      He hath been in unusual pleasure, and
      Sent forth great largesse to your offices.
      (Banquo to Macbeth: II, i, 14–16)

_____

_____

9.   They were suborned.
      Malcolm and Donalbain, the King's two sons,
      Are stolen away and fled, which puts upon them
      Suspicion of the deed. (Macduff's answer when Ross asks
      why the grooms would murder the King: II, iv, 31–34)

_____

_____

_____

10.   He is already named, and gone to Scone
     To be invested.
     (Macduff of Macbeth: II, iv, 39–40)

_____

_____

11.   God's benison go with you.
     (Old man's farewell: II, iv, 51)

_____

8. Elizabethan Word Bank—Part II

SENNET: a trumpet call often used to signal an entrance or an exit on the Elizabethan stage
VIZARDS: masks

CHARNEL HOUSE: a building into which bones were thrown when a grave was dug up to make room for a new corpse

AVAUNT: begone!

CAULDRON: a large kettle or pot

IMPRESS: to force

COZ: cousin; sometimes a courtesy title only

COLORS: a flag carried by a soldier

CLING: wither

SOOTH: truth

ORACLE: may be the person through whom a deity speaks OR may be information about the future given by an oracle

LAVE: to bathe

MAWS: bellies; stomachs

KITES: birds of prey, often hawks

SPECULATION: the power of sight

APPARITION: a ghostly figure

BODEMENTS: prophecies

SCHOOL: (verb) to teach; to discipline

AGUE: fever and chills

FORCED: reinforced

SIEGE: a military blockade of a town or fort in order to force its surrender

Paraphrase (rewrite in your own words) each of the following quotations from *Macbeth* to show the meaning clearly. Consult the Word Bank II vocabulary if you need help.

1. [Sennet sounded. Enter Macbeth, as King; Lady Macbeth, as
    Queen; Lennox, Ross, Lords, Ladies, and Attendants.]
    (Stage direction: III, i)

    _____

    _____

2.   If there come truth from them—
    As upon thee, Macbeth, their speeches shine—
    Why, by the verities (truths) on thee made good,
    May they not be my oracles as well
    And set me up in hope? (Banquo, to himself, thinking about
    the witches' prophecies: III, i, 6–10)

    _____

    _____

    _____

    _____

    _____

3.
. . . we
Must lave our honors in these flattering streams
And make our faces vizards to our hearts,
Disguising what they are. (Macbeth to Lady Macbeth, about
plans for Banquo: III, ii, 35–38)

_____

_____

_____

4.
If charnel houses and our graves must send
Those that we bury back, our monuments
Shall be the maws of kites.
(Macbeth when he sees a ghost: III, iv, 82–84)

_____

_____

_____

_____

5.
Avaunt! And quit my sight! Let the earth hide thee!
Thy bones are marrowless, thy blood is cold,
Thou hast no speculation in those eyes
Which thou dost glare with. (Macbeth to the ghost
mentioned in quotation 4 above: III, iv, 109–112)

_____

_____

_____

_____

6.
Round about the cauldron go.
In the poisoned entrails throw.
(entrails: internal parts of animals)
(One of the three witches: IV, i, 4–5)

_____

_____

7.
[Thunder. Third Apparition: Child crowned with a tree in his
hand.]
(Stage direction: IV, i, 93)

_____

_____

8.

    THIRD APPARITION: Macbeth shall never vanquished be until
        Great Birnam wood to high Dunsinane hill
        Shall come against him.
    MACBETH: That will never be.
        Who can impress the forest, bid the tree
        Unfix his earthbound root? Sweet bodements!
        Good!
        (IV, i, 101–106)

_____

_____

_____

_____

_____

9.

                                    My dearest coz,
        I pray you school yourself.
        (Ross to Lady Macduff: IV, ii, 17–18)

_____

_____

10.

    [Drum and colors. Enter Menteith, Caithness, Angus, Lennox,
    and Soldiers.]
    (Stage direction: V, ii)

_____

_____

11.

                         . . . our castle's strength
    Will laugh a siege to scorn. Here let them lie
    Till famine and the ague eat them up.
    Were they not forced with those that should be ours,
    We might have met them dareful, beard to beard,
    And beat them backward home. (Macbeth, as rebels prepare to
    lay siege to his fortress: V, v, 2–7)

_____

_____

_____

_____

_____

12.   If thou speak'st false,
Upon the next tree shalt thou hang alive
Till famine cling thee. If thy speech be sooth,
I care not if thou dost for me as much. (Macbeth to a
messenger who has brought bad news: V, v, 43–46)

_____

_____

_____

_____

9. Animal Lore

CATS: were often used as "familiars" (governing spirits of witches). "Graymalkin" was a popular name for a gray cat.

RAVENS: are large, glossy black birds. Frequently their croaking is associated with coming disaster and gloom.

OWL: is a nocturnal (active at night) bird of prey with a large head and large round eyes. It is a bird of ill-omen and its shriek suggests future disaster.

FALCON: is a kind of hawk used in hunting. It is reputed to be fierce. In the early stages of training, the falcon's eyes were "seeled": sewn shut to make it easier to handle. Later, the falcon was hooded until the moment of release for hunting.

TOADS: also were often used as "familiars" (governing spirits of witches). Notice that the witches quickly obey the call of their familiars. One toad familiar was called "Paddock."

MARTLET: is probably another name for house martin or swallow. The martlet is a bird that builds a small mud nest under the eaves of a *happy* house.

SNAKE: or serpent, is a reptile that has a reputation for sneakiness and treachery. Since its venom is sometimes fatal, it is also connected with death.

BEAR: in Shakespeare's time, bearbaiting was a popular entertainment. A bear was tied by a long rope to a stake. Large, ferocious dogs were encouraged to attack it.

Other animal images in *Macbeth:*
    a nest of scorpions
    a hell-kite eating chickens
    a tiger, a rhinoceros, and a bear
    a small wren fighting an owl
    a devouring vulture
    a swarm of insects

Answer the questions for each of the following quotations. Consult the Animal Lore vocabulary as necessary.

1.   The raven himself is hoarse
                     That croaks the fatal entrance of Duncan
                     Under my battlements.
                     (Lady Macbeth: I, v, 42–44)

Why does Lady Macbeth refer to a raven? Is Duncan going to have a good visit at
Macbeth's castle?

_____

_____

2.   This guest of summer,
                     The temple-haunting martlet, does approve
                     By his loved mansionry that the heaven's breath
                     Smells wooingly here . . . (Banquo to Duncan as they approach
                     Macbeth's castle: I, vi, 4–7)

What mood are Banquo and Duncan in as they approach Macbeth's castle for a visit?
Why does Banquo refer to the martlet?

_____

_____

3.   FIRST WITCH: I come, Graymalkin.
                     ALL: Paddock calls—anon!
                     (I, i, 9–10)

What does the brief bit of dialogue above show about the relationship between the
witches and their familiars?

_____

_____

4.   . . . look like the innocent flower
                     But be the serpent under it.
                     (I, v, 73–74)

Lady Macbeth says this to Macbeth just before the arrival of King Duncan. What ad-
vice is she giving her husband?

_____

_____

5.   MACBETH: I have done the deed. Didst thou not hear a noise?
                     LADY MACBETH: I heard the owl scream and crickets cry.
                     (II, ii, 16–17)

Why does Lady Macbeth refer to the owl screaming?

_____

Can you guess what the "deed" was that Macbeth referred to?

_____

6.
> We have scotched the snake, not killed it.
> She'll close and be herself, whilst our poor malice
> Remains in danger of her former tooth.
> (III, ii, 15–17)

Macbeth says this as he realizes that though he has killed the King, he is still surrounded by potential enemies. Keeping in mind that "scotched" means "wounded" and that "close" means "heal" or "unite or join," explain Macbeth's feelings at this time.

_____

_____

7.
> There the grown serpent lies. The worm that's fled
> Hath nature that in time will venom breed,
> No teeth for the present.
> (III, iv, 33–35)

Macbeth has ordered that a man be killed. The man is now dead, but the man's son escapes. What is Macbeth's fear? Why does he refer to a serpent?

_____

_____

8.
> 'Tis unnatural,
> Even like the deed that's done. On Tuesday last
> A falcon towering in her pride of place
> Was by a mousing owl hawked at and killed. (II, iv, 12–15)

Someone makes this comment after the murder of King Duncan. Why did Shakespeare use the reference to the falcon and owl?

_____

_____

9.
> Come, seeling night,
> Scarf up the tender eye of pitiful day,
> And with thy bloody and invisible hand
> Cancel and tear to pieces that great bond
> Which makes me pale! (III, ii, 51–55)

Macbeth is thinking of Banquo, his old friend, who now is threatening Macbeth's newly acquired crown. In fact, Banquo _is_ the "bond" that ties Macbeth, that keeps him from doing as he chooses. With this in mind, explain Macbeth's words above.

_____

_____

_____

10.
> They have tied me to a stake, I cannot fly,
> But bearlike I must fight the course.
> (V, vii, 1–2)

Macbeth says this to himself. What kind of situation do you think he finds himself in? Why the reference to a bear?

_____

_____

11. *For Discussion:* Look over all the animals and their traits on page 19. Think about them for a moment. How does Shakespeare use animal imagery in the play, *Macbeth?*

10. Military Words

BATTLEMENTS

A castle in Macbeth's time almost always had a *battlement:* a low wall, usually made of stone, built on top of the main wall. (See *EXTERIOR*) Since the main walls were very thick, they formed—inside the battlement—a *wall-walk* (see *INTERIOR*) where soldiers could patrol and from which they could shoot arrows at the attackers.

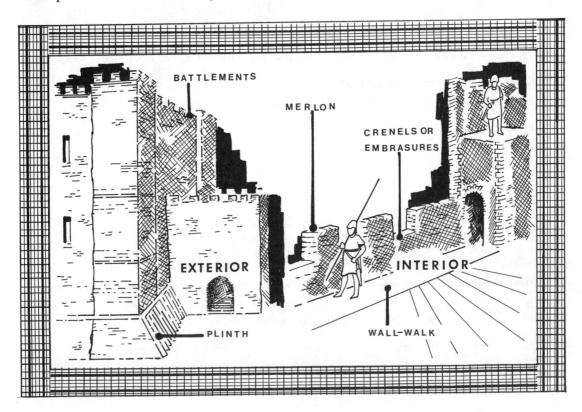

The solid sections of the battlement were called *merlons,* and defenders could find shelter behind them. The open sections were called *crenels* or *embrasures* and through them the defenders could fire cannon or discharge arrows on the enemy below.

A *list* was an enclosed space in which tournaments were held; a place of combat.

A *champion* was someone who fought against another individual in single combat. Usually he fought for someone or to protect someone.

To the utterance was a phrase used to indicate that the fight would be to the last extremity, that is—to death.

WEAPONS USED IN MACBETH'S TIME

STAVE: weapon with a long shaft and sharp head or blade
SWORD: weapon with a long blade for cutting or thrusting; also called a ''steel''; when not in use, it was ''sheathed'' in a ''scabbard.''
DAGGER: sharp, pointed knife, rather short; the handle was called the ''dudgeon.''
SHIELD: a broad piece of defensive armor carried on the arm

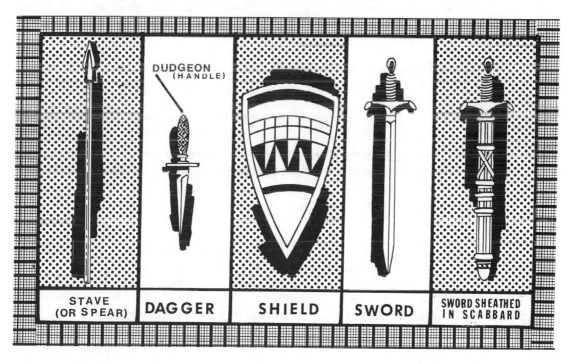

MISCELLANEOUS TERMS

UNSEAMED: ripped open
NAVE: navel
CHAPS: cheeks
KERNS: Irish soldiers who fought on foot
GALLOWGLASSES: Irish soldiers who fought on horseback

Answer the questions that follow the quotations below. Consult the vocabulary for military words as necessary.

1.
Why did you bring these daggers from the place?
They must lie there. Go carry them, and smear
The sleepy grooms with blood. (II, ii, 57–59) (Lady Macbeth to
Macbeth after the murder of Duncan.)

a. Who did the deed?

_____

b. With what weapon? What did the weapon look like?

_____

c. Who is to be blamed for the deed?

_____

2.
To Ireland, I. Our separated fortune
Shall keep us both the safer. Where we are
There's daggers in men's smiles. (II, iii, 161–163) (Donalbain to
his brother Malcolm who is headed for England after the
murder of their father, King Duncan.)

Explain the expression, "there's daggers in men's smiles."

_____

_____

3.
For brave Macbeth—well he deserves that name—
Disdaining fortune, with his brandished steel,
Which smoked with bloody execution,
Like valor's minion carved out his passage
Till he faced the slave,
Which ne'er shook hands, nor bade farewell to him,
Till he unseamed him from the nave to the chaps,
And fixed his head upon our battlements. (I, ii, 18–25)

Thus spoke the sergeant, a messenger from the battlefield, to King Duncan, describing Macbeth's fight with the rebel Macdonwald. The king then replied:

Oh, valiant Cousin! Worthy gentleman!

a. On the battlefield, what weapon did Macbeth use against Macdonwald?

_____

b. What did he do to him?

_____

c. How do both the sergeant and the king react to Macbeth's "bloody execution"?

_____

4.   The castle of Macduff I will surprise,
            Seize upon Fife, give to the edge o' the sword
            His wife, his babes, and all unfortunate souls
            That trace him in his line. (IV, i, 165–168) (Macbeth, to himself,
            as he considers his next step against Macduff.)

  a. What is "Fife"? (See page 1.)

_____

  b. What is Macbeth planning to do?

_____

5.   Be this the whetstone of your sword. Let grief
            Convert to anger, blunt not the heart, enrage it. (IV, iii, 265–266)
            (Malcolm to Macduff when they hear what has happened to
            Macduff's wife and children.)

A whetstone is a stone used to sharpen a blade. What does Malcolm mean?

_____

_____

6.   I cannot strike at wretched kerns whose arms
            Are hired to bear their staves. Either thou, Macbeth,
            Or else my sword, with an unbattered edge,
            I sheathe again undeeded. (V, vii, 21–24) (Macduff, facing
            Macbeth on the battlefield.)

Paraphrase these lines, making clear Macduff's intentions.

_____

_____

_____

_____

7.   Rather than so, come, fate, into the list,
            And champion me to the utterance! (III, i, 75–76) (Macbeth,
            remembering the witches promised Banquo that *his* sons
            would be kings.)

  a. What is Macbeth probably planning to do at this point?

_____

_____

  b. You probably know a bit about knights from the King Arthur stories. Why is it
     ironic for Macbeth to use these knightly terms at this time? (ironic: bitterly amusing)

_____

_____

8.   The raven himself is hoarse
That croaks the fatal entrance of Duncan
Under my battlements. (I, v, 42–44) (Lady Macbeth, as she awaits
the arrival of Duncan for an overnight stay in her castle.)

  a. What would we say today instead of ''battlements''?

    _____

  b. Why is ''battlements'' an effective word as it is used here?

    _____

9.   I'll fight till from my bones my flesh be hacked.
Give me my armor. (V, iii, 36–37) (Macbeth, as he begins to lose
hope.)

  a. What is Macbeth's attitude as his world begins to collapse around him?

    _____

  b. Why is the short sentence ''Give me my armor'' effective here?

    _____

10.   I have no words.
My voice is in my sword, thou bloodier villain
Than terms can give thee out! (V, viii, 8–10) (Macduff, as he
and Macbeth meet on the battlefield near the end of the play.)

  a. Why is Macduff so angry? (Review questions 5 and 6, if necessary.)

    _____

    _____

  b. What does Macduff mean when he says, ''My voice is in my sword''?

    _____

    _____

11. Words That Have Changed Their Meaning

Just to make life complicated, some words you think you know had different meanings in Shakespeare's time. To understand the play fully, you should be aware of these changes.

MINION: As usually used today, it refers to a servile dependent, to someone who depends on others. (A popular politician often has a battalion of ''minions''—people who run-and-fetch in return for favors.) But in Shakespeare's time, MINION meant ''darling'' or ''favorite.''

ILLNESS: In our time it means ''sickness.'' In Shakespeare's time it generally had a different meaning. It meant ''ill nature'' or ''evil nature.''

WEIRD: In our time *weird* means "odd" or "eerie" or "not real." From this meaning we get the modern slang term, "weirdo": someone who is extraordinarily strange. To Shakespeare, "weird" meant something more powerful: a description of someone who could control or influence one's fate or destiny. (Interestingly, this word appears in no other play by Shakespeare.)

LAVISH: Today *lavish* means "extravagant" or "luxurious." We talk about a "lavish" dinner or a "lavish" gift. To Shakespeare, it meant "insolent" or "overly bold."

MISSIVES: To us *missives* are "letters" or "notes." To Shakespeare, "missives" more often meant "messengers."

SECURITY: In our time it means "safety" or "freedom from care." Shakespeare often used it to mean "overconfident" or "careless."

GOUT: Today *gout* means a disease similar to arthritis. In Shakespeare's time, "gout" could also mean "a large splash or clot."

CLEAR: To us *clear* means "free of doubt" (a clear answer), or "transparent" (clear water). To Shakespeare, "clear" often meant "innocent", or even the adverb, "innocently."

After each of the following quotations, explain first what it seems to mean considering the present meaning of the word in italics. Then explain what it really means considering the use of the word in italics in Shakespeare's time.

Example:

When Macbeth and Lady Macbeth are planning to kill King Duncan, Lady Macbeth warns her husband to "look up *clear*."

    a. Present reading: Since "clear" today means "free of doubt," she seems to be telling him to have no doubts or fears.

    b. Past reading: Since "clear" to Shakespeare meant "innocent," she was actually telling him to "look innocent" . . . so that no one would suspect his intentions.

1. In reporting from the battlefield, Ross announced that Macbeth fought the rebel Macdonwald "arm 'gainst arm, Curbing his *lavish* spirit."

    a. _____

    _____

    b. _____

    _____

2. Lady Macbeth, when she first hears about the witches' prophecies, says to herself: "Whiles I stood rapt in the wonder of it, came *missives* from the king . . ."

    a. _____

    _____

    b. _____

    _____

3. Lady Macbeth, wondering if her husband will kill the king, muses:

> . . . thou wouldst be great;
> Are not without ambition, but without
> The *illness* should attend it . . .

a. _____

_____

b. _____

_____

4. Macbeth, seeing a vision of a dagger, while he is planning to murder the king, says:

> I see thee still;
> And on thy blade and dudgeon *gouts* of blood,
> Which was not so before.

(The "present reading" may seem nonsensical, but this can't be helped.)

a. _____

_____

b. _____

_____

5.

> And Duncan's horses—a thing most strange and certain—
> Beauteous and swift, the *minions* of their race,
> Turned wild in nature . . .

a. _____

_____

b. _____

_____

6. Banquo, remembering the witches' prophecies, says to himself:

> Thou hast it now: king, Cawdor, Glamis, all,
> As the *weird* women promis'd . . .

a. _____

_____

b. _____

_____

7. Says Hecate, the leader of the witches:

> And you all know *security*
> Is mortals' chiefest enemy.

a. _____

_____

b. _____

_____

12. Shakespeare's Language Legacy

Most of us use about 2800 words in our regular conversation and writing.

The King James version of the Bible uses 6,000 words.

Shakespeare—in his plays—used *19,000* words.

The man was a wordsmith, a word lover, a word builder—and we today still use the words he "built."

You speak Shakespeare often, whether you realize it or not. Have you ever talked of:

"the green-eyed monster"
"pomp and circumstance"
"a foregone conclusion"
"wear my heart on my sleeve"?

All are from *Othello*.

From *Hamlet:*
"flaming youth"
"in my mind's eye"
"method in his madness"
"the primrose path"

From *Julius Caesar:*
"it was Greek to me"
"a dish fit for the gods"
"an itching palm"
"a lean and hungry look"

From the *Henry* plays:
"give the devil his due"
"hearts of gold"
"he has eaten me out of house and home"
"the weaker vessel"

From *Romeo and Juliet:*
"a fool's paradise"

From *King John:*
"paint the lily"
"cold comfort"
"elbow room"

From *Much Ado About Nothing:*
"merry as the day is long"
"good men and true"

From *Macbeth*:

> "the milk of human kindness"
> "a sorry sight"
> "the crack of doom"
> "make assurance doubly sure"

And there are dozens more—all word combinations created by Shakespeare and now a part of our language.

But Shakespeare's real genius lay in making words work harder—in cajoling a word into doing something it had never done before—or even in creating new words. (We don't know, for sure, that Shakespeare created the words listed below, only that they are recorded for the first time in one of his plays.)

FRUGAL: (careful, sparing) used for the first time in *Merry Wives of Windsor* in 1600.

ACCOMMODATION: (room and provisions for visitors or guests) used for the first time in 1604 in *Othello*.

INDISTINGUISHABLE: (cannot be recognized as different from something else) used for the first time in *Troilus and Cressida* in 1602.

OBSCENE: (disgusting, abominable) used for the first time in *Richard II* in 1595.

ANIMAL: (as suggesting a brute or beast) used for the first time in *As You Like It* in 1599.

DWINDLE: (to become smaller and smaller) used for the first time in *Henry IV, Part I* in 1597; and for the second time in *Macbeth* in 1606.

HOMEKEEPING: (taking care of a home) used for the first time in *Two Gentlemen of Verona* in 1594.

LONELY: (having no companionship) used for the first time in *Coriolanus* in 1608.

DISLOCATE: (to displace a bone from its proper position) used for the first time in *King Lear* in 1605.

PREMEDITATED: (considered beforehand; deliberately planned) used for the first time in *A Midsummer Night's Dream* in 1595.

RELIANCE: (dependence on, confidence in) used for the first time in *Timon of Athens* in 1607.

Again, the list could go on and on.

Interesting, too, are Shakespeare-created words that have *not* lasted. Here are a few.

SMILET: a little smile
DISCANDY: melt
RAZORABLE: adjective for a boy about ready to be shaved
BIRTHDOM: native place
SUMMER'S TANLINGS: suntanned children

Perhaps some of them will still become part of our language. Wouldn't it be fun to notice a SMILET on someone's face, or to note (with a smirk) that young Jimmy is almost RAZORABLE?

Shakespeare, the wordsmith: almost as important a man as Shakespeare, the playwright.

QUESTIONS

1. Which "famous phrase" (pages 29–30) could you use in the following situations?

   a. Your sister is so jealous of her husband that she barely lets him out of her sight. You warn her to beware of "the _____."

   b. You have been thoroughly happy, but you suddenly realize that a person you thought was your friend isn't; that your money has all been spent; and that you have no way to get home. You realize that you have been living in "a _____ _____."

   c. You wish to warn someone not to try to make something beautiful still more beautiful. You say: "Don't _____."

2. a. In *Henry IV*, Part I, Falstaff, a hugely fat man, is trying to persuade a friend that he is suffering. He says: "Bardolph, am I not fallen away vilely since this last action? . . . Do I not dwindle? Why, my skin hangs about me like an old lady's loose gown." What, according to Falstaff, has happened to him? What does "dwindle" mean?

   _____

   b. In *Macbeth*, the first witch is laying a curse on a sailor. She chants:

   > Weary sennights nine times nine
   > Shall he dwindle, peak, and pine.

   Note: a "sennight" means seven nights or a week
   "peak" means grow thin
   What's going to happen to the sailor if the witch has her way? For how long is she going to plague him?

   _____

   _____

   c. Write an original sentence using the word "dwindle."

   _____

   _____

3. a. In *A MIDSUMMER NIGHT'S DREAM*, Theseus says:

   > Where I have come, great clerks have purposed
   > To greet me with premeditated welcomes . . .

   What is a premeditated welcome?

   _____

   b. What is the difference between a premeditated homicide and a non-premeditated homicide? Why is the former usually penalized more severely?

   _____

   _____

c. Write an original sentence using the word "premeditated."

_____

_____

4.a. Most of the time we use "frugal" in connection with money. A "frugal" person is someone who is careful with money, who spends as little as possible. But in *The Merry Wives of Windsor,* Shakespeare uses it in a different way. Mistress Page says: "I was then frugal of my mirth." What did she mean?

_____

_____

b. At the end of a play, your friend comments that you were "frugal with your applause." What does your friend mean?

_____

_____

c. Write an original sentence using the word "frugal."

_____

_____

5.a. In *King Lear,* a Gentleman says of Queen Cordelia: "Those happy smilets that played on her ripe lip . . . " What does this mean?

_____

_____

b. Write an original sentence using the word "smilets."

_____

_____

6.a. In *The Tempest,* Antonio talks of the Queen of Tunis who lives so far from Naples that she can receive no news from it "till newborn chins be rough and razorable." What does this mean?

_____

_____

b. Write an original sentence using the word "razorable."

_____

_____

7.a. In *Cymbeline,* Belarius muses that circumstances may force one who is gentle born to be denied the courtesy his birth promised and to become, instead, "hot summer's tanlings and the shrinking slaves of winter." What did he mean?

_____

_____

b. Write an original sentence using ''summer's tanling'' or ''summer's tanlings.''

_____

_____

8.a. In *Macbeth,* Macduff cries: ''Let us rather hold fast the mortal sword, and like good men, bestride our downfall'n birthdom.'' What was he exhorting his friends to do?

_____

_____

b. Write an original sentence using the word ''birthdom.''

_____

_____

9.a. In *Antony and Cleopatra,* Antony notices that those who fawned on him when he was powerful now ''do discandy, melt their sweets on blossoming Caesar.'' What did Antony mean?

_____

_____

b. Write an original sentence using the word ''discandy.''

_____

_____

EXPERIMENT IN LANGUAGE

10. As a class, choose ONE of the five words listed as Shakespearean failures: smilet; discandy; razorable; birthdom; summer's tanlings. (We recommend the first, the third, or the fifth.) Then attempt to make this word an accepted and recognized word in your school. Some possible approaches:
    a. Have a couple of students write ''Letters to the Editor'' (for the school newspaper) using the word in a nonchalant fashion. Do not define the word; let the context define it.
    b. Make a concerted effort to use the word at least once a week in conversation. If each of 25 students can do this, the word will be used 25 times each week and soon hundreds of people will have heard it.
    c. Develop a slogan that uses the word, but be sure the slogan is relevant to some issue important to your school. For example, if your school's drama department is putting on *Yankee Doodle Dandy,* you might come up with the slogan: ''Brag about your birthdom—see *Yankee Doodle Dandy.*''
    d. Brainstorm! Try to find other methods to use and publicize your word.

All of the above will take time—months, probably. But wouldn't it be exciting someday to see the word appear in your local newspaper, or even to hear it on television? *You,* then, would have helped to add a word to our language. You would, in a sense, have out-Shakespeared Shakespeare!

UNIT III

Stage and History

13. Shakespeare's Stage

Today the dinner theater is becoming increasingly popular: plays—usually comedies—presented inside a restaurant to the delight of diners. Interestingly enough, that's *almost* how the theater started in England eight centuries ago.

Plays were first presented in town squares and in empty lots, but in London they were soon switched to the courtyards of inns. In fact, the inn and its courtyard provided the blueprint for the first theater.

INN	EARLY THEATER
Rooms on all four sides of a courtyard opened onto galleries. In the courtyard, a platform on trestles acted as an impromptu stage.	Galleries were grouped around all four sides of a courtyard. A stage built at one end occupied about one-third of the courtyard area.
Inn guests paid the landlord and sat in the galleries.	"Rich" spectators paid two pennies to sit in the upper galleries, three pennies to sit in the lower one.
People from outside the inn paid the actors and *stood* in the courtyard.	Commoners (the "ordinary" people) *stood* in the courtyard, called "the pit," and paid one penny. These spectators, called "*ground*lings," were boisterous.
At one end of the courtyard were the stables.	In British theaters, even today, the main floor is called "the stalls."

The Globe Theater (Shakespeare's favorite) was octagonal (eight-sided). The rear three sides were used by the players, the other five by spectators.

Most plays lasted two hours. With no intermission and no time-outs for scene shifting, the tempo was fast. Audiences were strongly involved.

Each theater had a cast of 25–30 actors. Plays were written with these individuals in mind. Female parts were played by boys. Each company had a "clown" who provided comic relief.

Little scenery was used. Settings were evoked by *words*. Occasionally special properties (props) helped. A watchman with a lantern signaled that it was night; smoke sent up through the trap provided fog; flashes of gunpowder provided lightning.

As you can see from the sketch of the Globe Playhouse, the Elizabethan theater was quite different from the modern theater.

Notice:

STUDY: a sort of inner stage, suitable for "small" scenes, like the tomb scene in *Romeo and Juliet.*

TARRAS: (terrace) often used for battlement scenes.

POSTS: supporting a canopy—a blue canopy that represented the sky, or the heavens. The posts also served as trees, masts, etc.

HUTS: above the sky (or heavens) where the backstage crew could lower gods and goddesses.

TRAP: in the middle of the platform, through which devils or witches could appear or disappear.

TURRET: (tower) housed a bell. Here, other sound effects—cannon, drums, trumpets, etc.—were created.

PLATFORM: Notice the shape of the platform. In our theater, the stage is usually at one end of a hall with the audience seated in front of it. In the Elizabethan theater, the platform-stage protruded well into the audience. Actors were often surrounded on three sides by spectators.

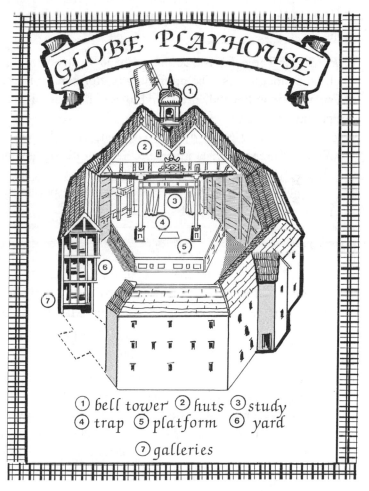

① bell tower ② huts ③ study
④ trap ⑤ platform ⑥ yard
⑦ galleries

Take a good long look at the plan of the Elizabethan theater. Some of its characteristics are important to the reading of any Shakespearean play—and therefore of *Macbeth*.

QUESTIONS

1. Where did a banquet scene probably take place? (Use the sketch plus common sense.)

   _____

2. How was the witches' cauldron probably hoisted onto the stage?

   _____

3. Where did Macbeth and Lady Macbeth probably stand when they were discussing the murder of the King?

   _____

4. Where did the battlefield scenes probably take place?

   _____

Two conventions of Elizabethan drama are closely connected to the physical structure of the theater.

THE ASIDE: The *aside* is a comment made by an actor. It is heard by the audience but not by the other actors. The protruding platform made it easy for the actor to step to one side, wink at the audience (maybe), and make a sarcastic, witty, or simply explanatory comment.

THE SOLILOQUY: A *soliloquy* is a dramatic monologue (monologue: speech by one actor alone on the stage) that gives the illusion of being a character's unspoken thoughts. When an actor spoke a soliloquy, he probably stepped forward, moving close to the audience, away from his fellow actors. It is important to remember that a soliloquy represents the *thoughts* of a character.

QUESTIONS

5. In Act I, Scene iii, Macbeth has just heard from the witches that he is Thane of Glamis, will be Thane of Cawdor, and will be King hereafter. Messengers arrive to tell him he has just been named Cawdor. Macbeth turns away with an *aside:*

   > Glamis, and Thane of Cawdor.
   > The greatest is behind.

   ("Behind" here means "yet to come.") A moment later, he turns to the messengers and says: "Thanks for your pains." He then goes on to talk with Banquo. But only the audience heard the aside, only they (not the other characters) know Macbeth's thoughts at this moment. What were Macbeth's thoughts? Why did he speak them in an aside, not to one of the other characters?

   _____

   _____

   _____

   _____

36

6. After Macbeth and Lady Macbeth have decided that King Duncan must be killed, Macbeth broods about it. Should he? Or shouldn't he? He would like to be King—but murder? Murder of a kinsman? Murder of a guest? Imagine the scene. Macbeth is alone. He is edgy; his conscience is already beginning to torment him. If he is to do the deed, it must be done *now*. He speaks his thoughts—in a well-known soliloquy. Read it, preferably aloud.

> Is this a dagger which I see before me,
> The handle toward my hand? Come, let me clutch thee.
> I have thee not, and yet I see thee still.
> Art thou not, fatal vision, sensible
> To feeling as to sight? Or art thou but
> A dagger of the mind, a false creation,
> Proceeding from the heat-oppressed brain?
> I see thee yet, in form as palpable
> As this which now I draw.
> Thou marshal'st me the way that I was going,
> And such an instrument I was to use.
> Mine eyes are made the fools o' the other senses,
> Or else worth all the rest. I see thee still,
> And on thy blade and dudgeon gouts of blood,
> Which was not so before. There's no such thing.
> It is the bloody business which informs
> Thus to mine eyes. (II, i, 41–57)

Here is a brief glossary to help you:

SENSIBLE: able to be felt   MARSHAL'ST: leads, conducts
PALPABLE: clear, obvious   INFORMS: creates forms

Read the soliloquy once more. Will Macbeth do the deed? Will his conscience later bother him? What does the soliloquy tell you about Macbeth and the way his mind works?

_____

_____

_____

_____

7. Films (movies and TV productions) have a different way of handling soliloquies. They usually show a close-up of the character in an almost trance-like state. The lips are not moving; the voice seems to come from a distance. It is clear that we are in the mind of the character. Compare the two methods: the Elizabethan and the modern. Can you think of one advantage of each? Which do *you* prefer?

_____

_____

_____

_____

14. Equivocation

"Nothing is, but what is not."

Parent: "What time did you get in last night?"

You (an equivocating teenager): "Well, we left the Civic Center
at eleven, and it's only a half hour drive, so there was
plenty of time to be in by midnight."

Were you home by midnight? You neglected to mention that you stopped for pizza and took the long way home. You didn't actually lie, but you deliberately tried to mislead your parent into believing something not true—that you met your curfew.

The above is an example of *equivocation:* the art of misleading, usually through language.

An *equivocator* is a person who tries to mislead through language.

To equivocate means to try to mislead through language.

Equivocal is a statement or event that is open to two or more interpretations and is usually intended to mislead.

The two major elements of *equivocation* are:

    1. A lie is not actually told

    2. The truth is not told either, but a false idea is deliberately fostered.

Why all this talk about *equivocation?* Because *Macbeth* is a play based on it. Macbeth equivocates; so do the witches; so does Lady Macbeth. Equivocation is everywhere; the atmosphere is thick with it. The action is motivated by it.

If you hope to understand this play, keep *equivocation* in mind. Be alert for it, and be prepared *by* it.

Between 1598 and 1606, in England, there was much talk of equivocation. The Gunpowder Plot, a conspiracy to blow up Parliament, had failed, and the conspirators had been arrested. One of them, Father Garnet, a Jesuit, used equivocation during the trial. He was found guilty anyway and sentenced to death, but before he died, he claimed that equivocation is sometimes justified. England promptly split into "for" and "against" groups, and the word "equivocation" was on everyone's lips.

In the play, *Macbeth,* equivocation begins on the next to last line of the first scene. The three witches are huddled on a heath, amid thunder and lightning. The witches chant:

Fair is foul, and foul is fair . . .

The day is indeed "fair" for Macbeth and Banquo, leaders of the king's forces, for they have defeated the rebels on the battlefield. But the day is also "foul," for thunder is raging and lightning streaks across the sky. So "fair" and "foul," opposite in meaning, seem to become equal. The witches here set the stage: little is as it *seems* to be.

QUESTIONS

    1. The witches predict that Macbeth will be thane (lord) of Cawdor, and then king. Al-

most immediately messengers enter to tell Macbeth he has been proclaimed thane of Cawdor. He steps aside and muses:

> [*Aside*]   This supernatural soliciting
> Cannot be ill; cannot be good: if ill,
> Why hath it given me earnest of success,
> Commencing in a truth? I am thane of Cawdor:
> If good, why do I yield to that suggestion
> Whose horrid image doth unfix my hair
> And make my seated heart knock at my ribs,
> Against the use of nature? (I, iii, 138–145)

(Remember: "ill" in Shakespeare's time meant "evil." "Soliciting" meant "tempting." "Against the use of nature" meant "in an unnatural way." "Earnest" meant "evidence." "Unfix my hair" meant "make my hair stand on end."

a. Read the passage several times. Then *paraphrase* it: that is, express it in your own words, making the meaning clear.

_____

_____

_____

_____

_____

_____

_____

_____

b. Macbeth says that the supernatural temptation cannot be evil or good.

1. Why does he say it cannot be evil?

_____

2. Why does he say it cannot be good?

_____

3. Do both answers seem equally logical, equally valid?

_____

4. With the answers to the above three questions in mind, answer: How are Macbeth's thoughts an example of equivocation?

_____

_____

_____

2. On the night King Duncan was murdered, the porter who guards the castle gate has been drinking heavily and imagines himself the gatekeeper of hell. When he hears a

knock, he grumbles: "Who's there?" Then he guesses that it might be a farmer who hanged himself because of the low prices of farm products. There's a second knock, and he guesses it's an equivocator. There's a third knock, and he guesses it's a tailor who cheats his customers. Then he decides it's too cold to be hell, after all. "I'll devil-porter it no further," he mutters and goes to open the gate.

a. According to the passage, what are three types of people who might be condemned to hell?

_____

_____

b. Why, in your opinion, did Shakespeare choose to open this scene (II, iii) with the drunken porter's imaginings?

_____

_____

_____

_____

When you read the play, look for equivocation especially in the witches' prophecies. Then use your wits to see if you are smarter than Macbeth!

15. The "News" in Macbeth

Like any good writer, Shakespeare had his eyes and his ears open and alert at all times. He saw, and he heard, and he read. And all that he saw and heard and read was tucked away in his subconscious, ready to be called up as needed.

Here are a few of the news items Shakespeare must have come across in the months preceding the writing of *Macbeth*. (Remember: *Macbeth* was first performed at Hampton Court on August 7, 1606.)

ITEM: King James loved to hunt with hounds so, in 1605, he sent a message to all his nobles *suggesting* they supply him with dogs, but only with the *right* kind. Most did, and many also sent a letter—a catalog or file—describing the fine points of each dog offered. These were "hounds" trained to hunt and kill. For months the court talked of little else but hunting with hounds, a cruel sport that Shakespeare disliked. He seldom used references to hounds in his plays but, in 1606, he did, in *Macbeth*.

ITEM: On March 28, 1606, Father Garnet was found guilty of conspiracy (in the Gunpowder Plot) and was sentenced to death. On the very next day, March 29th, one of the worst hurricanes of all time hit England and the western European countries. Here is an early account:

> . . . the wind was so extraordinarily great and
> violent, that it caused great shipwrecks in En-
> gland, Scotland, France, and the Low Countries.
> It blew down part of the Hugonot church at Diope,
> and divers other churches in the lower Belgia,
> and in Germany, in every of which said places,
> and some others it blew down villages, trees, and
> windmills; it also caused the Sea, and divers
> Rivers to overflow their boundes, and drowned
> many people, and much cattle.

In another account, we hear of a steeple being blown down, killing eighty people. (A steeple at that time was sometimes called a "pyramid.")

Many people felt Garnet was under the protection of the Devil, who sent the hurricane, as a punishment, when Garnet was sentenced to death.

ITEM: King Christian of Denmark (King James's brother-in-law) arrived in London on July 7, 1606, for a long visit. Approaching London, the Danish ships fired double cannons in a joyous salute. In August, the two kings visited the Tower of London, and King Christian himself fired a cannon. Especially loud discharges were called "double cracks." (Cannon existed in Shakespeare's time but not in 1040 when *Macbeth* takes place.)

ITEM: During his visit, King Christian distributed largesse (gifts) to the court, including $10,000 to the officers "above the stairs." William Shakespeare was a groom of the outer chamber and therefore received a share of this $10,000. (The silver dollar was first coined in 1518 in Bohemia and called a "thaler." It became popular in Europe and was occasionally used in England where "thaler" became "dollar." After King Christian's visit in 1606, the dollar became more popular in England. This "dollar" is not the same as the U.S. dollar.)

ITEM: James I liked to consider himself a doctor capable of healing his nation's ills. In 1604 (two years before Shakespeare wrote *Macbeth*) James published "Counterblast to Tobacco." In the preface, he wrote that it is a king's duty "to purge it (the nation) of all those diseases, by medicines meet for the same." Shakespeare certainly read the king's booklet and in *Macbeth* used the image four times.

ITEM: Common in England during the medieval and Elizabethan periods was the king's evil: scrofula, a "tubercular infection of the glands and bones of the neck caused by drinking milk from infected cattle." Starting with Edward the Confessor, the monarchs of England for hundreds of years "cured" scrofula patients by touching them and crossing their sores with an "angel"—a special gold coin minted for this purpose. James was reluctant to continue the custom so, in *Macbeth*, Shakespeare modified the procedure. It is said that, after seeing the play, James accepted Shakespeare's suggestion and began hanging specially minted "angels" around the patients' necks as he prayed for them.

1. Macbeth (III, i, 99–108) is talking with some hired murderers. They insist they are "men", and Macbeth retorts:

> Aye, in the catalogue ye go for men;
> As hounds and greyhounds, mongrels, spaniels, curs,
> Shoughs, water-rugs and demi-wolves, are clept (called)
> All by the name of dogs . . .

  a. What analogy (comparison) is Shakespeare making between "men" and "dogs?"

_____

_____

Macbeth then goes on:

>   . . . the valued file
> Distinguishes the swift, the slow, the subtle,
> The housekeeper, the hunter, every one
> According to the gift which bounteous nature
> Hath in him clos'd, whereby he does receive
> Particular addition*, from the bill
> That writes them all alike; and so of men.

(*Addition: In the 17th century, "addition" was a word or group of words that helped to identify someone by indicating trade, residence, or social rank. Example: John Brown, barber; "barber" was an addition that helped to identify this particular John Brown.)

  b. How does this passage, as well as the preceding one, reflect on subjects of interest to King James?

_____

_____

  c. In Act V, Scene viii, line 4 (near the end of the play) Macduff, finding Macbeth on the battlefield, shouts: "Turn, hell-hound, turn!"
(Hell-hound: a guard dog for the gates of hell; a fiendish person.)
Why does he use this particular epithet, or name, for Macbeth?

_____

_____

2. When Macbeth meets a second time with the witches, he demands to know what the future holds for him. They hesitate, and he speaks angrily:

> Though you untie the winds and let them fight
> Against the churches! though the yesty waves
> Confound and swallow navigation up;
> Though bladed corn be lodg'd and trees blown down;
> Though castles topple on their warders' heads;
> Though palaces and pyramids do slope

Their heads to their foundations; though the treasure
Of nature's germens (seeds) tumble all together,
Even till destruction sicken; answer me
To what I ask you. (IV, i, 53–62)

a. Read again the account of the 1606 hurricane in England. What specific details appear both in the Shakespearean passage and in the news account?

_____

_____

_____

_____

b. Why is Macbeth, at this point in the play, describing the destruction caused by the hurricane?

_____

_____

c. What does this passage tell us about Macbeth's willingness to deal with evil, even with the evil of hell?

_____

_____

3. Lady Macbeth has been walking in her sleep, and a doctor has been summoned to examine her. He says he can do little for her. Macbeth says:

                    If thou couldst, doctor, cast
    The water of my land*, find her disease,
    And purge it to a sound and pristine health,
    I would applaud thee to the very echo,
    That should applaud again. Pull 't off, I say.
    What rhubarb, senna, or what purgative drug,
    Would scour these English hence? (V, iii, 58–64)
    (*perform a diagnosis)

a. What is Macbeth asking the doctor to do (though he knows it's impossible)?

_____

_____

b. How does this speech reflect an interest of King James?

_____

_____

4. When Malcolm and Macduff visit King Edward's court, in England, a doctor tells them the king will be delayed for he is "touching for the king's evil." Malcolm and Macduff discuss this.

MACDUFF: What's the disease he means?
MALCOLM: 'Tis call'd the evil:
    A most miraculous work in this good king;
    Which often, since my here-remain in England,
    I have seen him do. How he solicits heaven,
    Himself best knows: but strangely-visited people,
    All swol'n and ulcerous, pitiful to the eye,
    The mere despair of surgery, he cures,
    Hanging a golden stamp about their necks,
    Put on with holy prayers: and 'tis spoken,
    To the succeeding royalty he leaves
    The healing benediction. (IV, iii, 162–173)

a. What is the "king's evil"? How, apparently, could it be cured?

_____

_____

b. What modification of the "cure" does Shakespeare make?

_____

_____

c. How does the king acquire this special gift for healing this disease?

_____

_____

5. An *anachronism* is an error in chronology—a misplacement of an event or person or object in time. For example, if you wrote a story set in 1800 and you had a character drive a car, this would be an anachronism. If someone (in the same story) mentioned our current president, this too would be an anachronism.

a. Early in the play, a sergeant reports that Macbeth and Banquo fought like "cannons overcharg'd with double cracks." (I, ii, 41) Why is Shakespeare's reference to "cannon" an anachronism?

_____

    This passage was added just before the first performance of the play. Suggest a reason why Shakespeare added it.

_____

_____

b. Ross mentions that the Scots would not let Norway's king bury his dead:

        Till he disbursed, at Saint Colme's inch*,
        Ten thousand dollars to our general use. (I, ii, 70–71)

(*St. Colme's inch: the island of St. Columba in the Firth of Forth.)
In Shakespeare's source for Macbeth, no specific amount of money is mentioned.

Suggest a reason why Shakespeare specified $10,000. Why is the reference to $10,000 an anachronism?

_____

This passage, too, was inserted just before the performance. Suggest a reason for its inclusion.

_____

_____

6. In truth, it wasn't the Norwegians who helped the rebels in 1040. It was the Danes. In your opinion, why did Shakespeare change "Danes" to "Norwegians"? (I, ii)

_____

_____

7. Considering your answers to 1–6, would you conclude that William Shakespeare was strongly influenced by the world in which he lived? Just for fun, ask yourself: if Shakespeare were alive today, what modern events and ideas might he refer to in his writing?

Examples:

The space race, for sure. Shakespeare might have viewed it as an indication of the arrogance of human beings and of the end of the world; or he might have seen it as a reflection of the power of some ruler.

The computer. Maybe Shakespeare would have used it as he did witches: to feed in data and to ask for predictions. Probably he would have used computer terminology: perhaps Malcolm would have been described as a "print-out" of King Duncan; Macbeth (or Lady Macbeth) would have been a "hacker."

_____

_____

_____

_____

_____

_____

_____

16. The Order of the Universe

Here is a technique that will help you to view the world in the same way the people in Shakespeare's day viewed it.

Imagine all the people in the world clustered together in the center of the universe.

Next, imagine all other things, both animate and inanimate, as tiny mirrors circling around these people.

When *one* person in the center commits a murder, that murder is reflected in every tiny mirror—with devastating effect. Storms rise and flood whole cities. Winds topple steeples. Horses eat horses, and owls turn on falcons. All Nature goes awry because some *one*—one human being—performed an unnatural and depraved act.

In daily life in the 20th century, many of us occasionally talk as though we believed in a cause-and-effect relationship between people and nature, but most of us don't really believe it.

In the Elizabethan period, people *did* accept this theory, fervently and completely.

If humans were wicked, Nature would be wicked, too.

If humans committed heinous deeds, nature would follow suit.

As you read *Macbeth,* watch for this correlation.

Watch:

the weather,

the birds, and

the animals . . .

as they related to human behavior.

Notice, too, the dramatic effect of this correlation. It seems *right* that a murder should be orchestrated to thunder and lightning—that treason should be played out against chaos in the animal world. It seems so right that we still use the technique today, though we no longer believe in this particular "Order of the Universe."

The next time you watch television (or read a story), be alert for these special Elizabethan echoes.

QUESTIONS

1. In "The Devil and Daniel Webster," a short story by Stephen Vincent Benet, the devil visits the home of Jabez Stone. The story goes on:

> . . . the dog took one look at the stranger and
> ran away howling, with his tail between his legs.

How is this an "Elizabethan echo"?

_____

_____

2. In "The Snows of Kilimanjaro," a short story by Ernest Hemingway, a man is seriously injured. He may be dying. This description is given.

> The cot the man lay on was in the wide shade of a
> mimosa tree and as he looked out past the shade onto
> the glare of the plain there were three of the big
> birds squatted obscenely, while in the sky, a dozen
> more sailed, making quick-moving shadows as they
> passed.

What kind of bird is referred to? How is this an "Elizabethan echo"?

_____

_____

3. You probably have seen dozens of reruns of the TV series, "Little House on the Prairie." It is about a close and loving family that faces many problems but each show ends happily. Each show opens and closes with the same scene: the sun is shining, the sky is blue, and a little girl, laughing happily, runs through the tall grass. How is this an example of the "Elizabethan echo"?

_____

_____

4. In the movie, "The Wizard of Oz," Dorothy and her dog Toto start in Kansas and somehow end in the Land of Oz. They meet the Munchkins, the Wicked Witch of the East, the Tin Woodman, the Scarecrow, and the Cowardly Lion. The world of Oz is a topsy-turvy world where little is as it seems. Why is it logical (from an Elizabethan point of view) that the story begins with a cyclone?

_____

_____

_____

5. Now shift into reverse. If _you_ were writing a story about two small children lost in a forest at night, what kind of weather would you provide? What animals or birds? Explain the reasons for your choices.

_____

_____

_____

_____

_____

6. Still in reverse. This time you are writing a TV script about a young man, severely handicapped, who still managed to place in the Olympics. Your script will be about the day of the race (and the young man will win the gold.) What kind of weather will you have? Will you use any animals or birds, directly or as images? Explain your choices.

_____

_____

_____

_____

_____

Writing Techniques

17. Alliteration

> Seven silly sisters swam swiftly in the strait,
> Forty feeble fillies flirted feverishly with Fate.

That's *alliteration*—alliteration gone wild, but alliteration all the same. Alliteration is the use of two or more words with the same initial sound. Shakespeare used it—more subtly, of course, but constantly and with conscious effect.

1. First, remember: initial sounds count, *not* initial letters. In each of the following clusters, identify the word that is *not* alliterative.

   compose - continue - cease - came
   kick - knee - kindergarten - keen
   eight - eat - either - Eden
   great - gnaws - gorgeous - gown

   gnat - never - gnome - glove
   Philadelphia - patriot - fix - pharmacy
   sigh - psychic - psalm - patter
   Charles - chow - chorus - choice

2. Next, try writing an alliterative couplet of your own. (See the one that begins this chapter.) Some easy-to-rhyme words for the ends of the two lines:

   > gloom (broom - room - doom - groom - tomb - whom - assume)
   > said (head - dead - red - fed - Ned - thread - sped)
   > flame (name - game - blame - came - dame - aim - fame)

3. Here are three quotations from *Macbeth*. Underline the alliterative words in each. (There may be more than one example of alliteration in a particular quotation.)
   a. Fair is foul, and foul is fair.
      Hover through the fog and filthy air. (I,i,11–12)
   b.   So should he look
      That seems to speak things strange. (I,ii,51–52)
   c. False face must hide what the false heart doth know. (I,vii,92)

4. On page 49 are incomplete phrases from *Macbeth*. Following the phrases are five adjectives. Match the adjectives and the incomplete phrases.

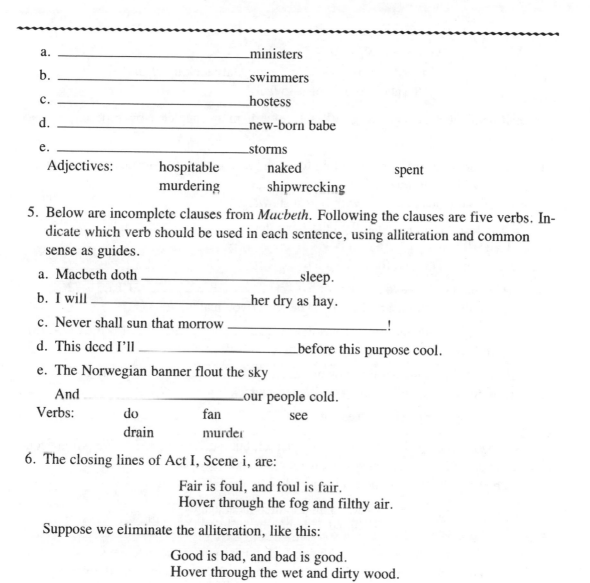

a. _____ministers

b. _____swimmers

c. _____hostess

d. _____new-born babe

e. _____storms

Adjectives: hospitable naked spent
  murdering shipwrecking

5. Below are incomplete clauses from *Macbeth*. Following the clauses are five verbs. Indicate which verb should be used in each sentence, using alliteration and common sense as guides.

a. Macbeth doth _____sleep.

b. I will _____her dry as hay.

c. Never shall sun that morrow _____!

d. This deed I'll _____before this purpose cool.

e. The Norwegian banner flout the sky

And _____our people cold.

Verbs: do fan see
  drain murder

6. The closing lines of Act I, Scene i, are:

> Fair is foul, and foul is fair.
> Hover through the fog and filthy air.

Suppose we eliminate the alliteration, like this:

> Good is bad, and bad is good.
> Hover through the wet and dirty wood.

Read both couplets aloud. They say *almost* the same thing, yet the effect of each is very different. Now *chant* each couplet. How does alliteration affect meaning?

18. Rhymed Couplets

The Elizabethan theater had no curtain with which to signal the end of a scene. Instead, playwrights often provided a signal: a rhyming couplet. You have already examined the closing couplet of Act I, Scene i.

> Fair is foul, and foul is *fair*.
> Hover through the fog and filthy *air*.

Sometimes a couplet is split between the speeches of two characters, as happens at the end of Act I, Scene v.

MACBETH: We will speak further.

LADY MACBETH: Only look up *clear*,
        To alter favor ever is to *fear*.

Read both couplets aloud to get a "feel" of a rhyming couplet. Now proceed to the exercise below.

1. "Play" Shakespeare—by providing for each blank a word that makes sense *and* that rhymes with the last word of the preceding line.

   a. Away, and mock the time with fairest show:

      False face must hide what the false heart doth _____.
      (I,vii,91–92)

   b. Hear it not, Duncan, for it is a knell

      That summons thee to heaven, or to _____. (II,i,71–72)

   c. Put on their instruments. Receive what cheer you may;

      The night is long that never finds the _____. (IV,iii,277–278)

   d. Were I from Dunsinane away and clear,

      Profit again should hardly draw me _____. (V,iii,70–71)

   e. Ring the alarum-bell! Blow, wind! come, wrack!

      At least we'll die with harness on our _____. (V,v,56–57)

2. Not every scene ends with a rhyming couplet, but most do. In *Macbeth* rhyming couplets appear at another time: when the three witches are on stage.

      The first two lines of the play are spoken by the First Witch:

                   When shall we three meet again
                   In thunder, lightning, or in rain?

   (Notice that the rhyme may seem imperfect, unless you pronounce the second syllable of "again" with a long **a,** as in "pain" or "make." Some imperfect rhymes are the result of changes of pronunciation since Shakespeare's day; others may be deliberate to prevent a singsong effect.)

      The Second Witch speaks; *you* complete the rhyming couplet.

                   When the hurlyburly's done
                   When the battle's lost and _____.

   And the Third Witch tosses in a single line which rhymes with the two above:

                   That will be ere the set of _____.

   The First Witch breaks in:

                   Where the place?

   The Second Witch answers:

                   Upon the heath.

The Third Witch notes smugly:

> There to meet with _____. (Insert from the play a proper
> name that *almost* rhymes with ''heath.'')

There you have it—most of the first scene—in rhyming couplets, possibly to increase the eerie effect of the witches, possibly to set the scene off from the rest of the play.

Later, in Act IV, Scene i, the witches meet again. And again their conversation is in rhyming couplets. The most famous rhyming couplet of all is repeated several times:

> Double, double toil and trouble;
> Fire burn and cauldron _____.

(Clue: what do the contents of a cauldron do when the cauldron has been over a fire for a long time?)

Make sure you have the last word right, then memorize the couplet. It will take only a few seconds and you will forever remember what a rhyming couplet is. (Besides, when you're furious and weighed down with problems, mutter these lines—and you will be magically comforted!)

19. Verse

Try reading the following nonsense verse aloud. Emphasize the second syllable in each foot. (The feet are separated by slash marks.) Example: ''When Arch'' is a foot; stress ''Arch.''

> When Arch/ ie found/ some coins,/ his stom/ ach spoke:
> He bought/ a piz/ za rich/ with cheese/ and sauce.
> It drib/ bled on/ his shirt/ and left/ red scars
> A cross/ his chin,/ it gummed/ his teeth,/ and hot
> Pink pep/ pers stung/ his tongue;/ it turned/ his hands
> To slabs/ of glue;/ it caught/ stray wisps/ of hair
> And paint/ ed them/ tom a/ to red./ Then, too,
> It gave/ him in/ di ges/ tion. So,/ he sighed,
> Then burped,/ and gulped/ some more./ ''What fun!''/ he cried.

What you just read is an exercise in *iambic pentameter,* the verse form favored by Shakespeare.

IAMB: two syllables, one unstressed, one stressed, in each foot
PENTAMETER: five feet
IAMBIC PENTAMETER: (eye AM bic pen TAM uh ter) five iambic feet

Iambic pentameter is the most natural verse form in English. Read the example several times at the beginning of this chapter, and you may even begin to *think* in iambic pentameter!

As an experiment, try developing one line of iambic pentameter. Let someone else provide a second, follow-up line; a third person, a third line, and so on. You should find this a fairly easy experiment because *iambic pentameter* is a *natural* rhythm.

Now that you know what *iambic pentameter* is, you can begin to recognize it in *Macbeth*. But first turn back to the "pizza poem."

Notice:

> That some lines end with natural pauses (lines 1 and 2, for example)
>
> That some lines do *not* end with natural pauses; instead, the sentence continues smoothly onto the next line (lines 3 and 4, for example)
>
> That the last two lines rhyme, forming a rhyming couplet (just as Shakespeare used rhyming couplets to end many of his scenes)
>
> That alliteration is used throughout the nine lines (lines 1 and 5, for example)
>
> That internal rhyme is used a couple of times ("stung" and "tongue" on line 5; "glue", line 6, and "too", line 7)

Read the nine lines of verse aloud once more, lightly emphasizing the second syllable of each foot but pausing only when the punctuation demands it (a colon, a semicolon, a period, and—to a lesser extent—a comma.)

By now, you should be getting the *feel* of *iambic pentameter*.

Now, to work.

After hearing that Duncan has appointed his elder son his heir, Macbeth (in an aside) muses:

> The Prince of Cumberland! that is a step
> On which I must fall down, or else o'erleap,
> For in my way it lies. Stars, hide your fires;
> Let not light see my black and deep desires:
> The eye wink at the hand; yet let that be
> Which the eye fears, when it is done, to see. (I,iv,55–60)

1. Read the first two and a half lines aloud, stressing every *second* syllable. So far, this is perfect iambic pentameter.

2. Now look at the second half of the third line: the fourth foot—"Stars, hide"—really contains two stressed syllables. It is a deliberate imperfection: one meant to jolt the reader and to vary the rhythm. Look at the fifth foot—"your fires." Once again we're back to the unstressed-stressed pattern; but the last word, "fires", contains an extra weak syllable at the end. Emphasize "fi" and let the "res" (pronounced "erz") taper off.

3. Read the first three lines aloud. Can you hear the basic rhythm? Add the fourth line. The only variation here is in the last foot. Again there is an extra syllable—the "res" ending. Read the first four lines aloud.

4. The fifth line is perfect iambic pentameter. The sixth varies in the first two feet. Stress "Which"—move quickly over "the" and "eye"—stress "fears." The rest of the line follows the iambic pentameter pattern.

5. Now put together all six lines. Read them aloud. Better yet, read them several times until you *feel* the iambic pentameter rhythm and the occasional variations.

Question: Did Shakespeare plan each line, each metrical foot? Did he search for unstressed/stressed syllables to follow the pattern?

Answer: Of course not. After getting the *feel* of iambic pentameter, any writer will find that it almost flows of its own volition. Try it. Write a couplet in iambic pentameter on any topic.

_____

_____

One more note. Sometimes an iambic pentameter line is broken and shared by two speakers. After the witches make their first prophecies, Macbeth turns to Banquo and says:

Your children shall be kings.

Banquo comments, probably emphasizing the first word:

You shall be king.

The two speeches together form one line of iambic pentameter. Read them aloud, with one person speaking for Macbeth and a different person for Banquo. Notice how the basic rhythm holds.

Question: Do *you* have to be constantly aware of iambic pentameter—of what it is—of where variations occur?

Answer: Of course not. After getting the *feel* of it, you will find it a natural rhythm, one easy to follow without thought . . . much as you follow the rhythm of your favorite pop singer.

Feeling the rhythm of Shakespeare's writing will help you to enjoy his style and understand his words. It may even, in a subtle way, improve the rhythm of your own speech and writing.

20. Allusions

If someone said you were as funny as *Bill Cosby,* you'd be delighted. You would know immediately that the person considered you a true comic—someone who knows how to laugh and how to make others laugh.

If an acquaintance who had been arrested said the experience had given him a taste of *hell,* you would understand exactly how he felt, because you know *hell* is a place of exquisite torment.

In both cases an *allusion* helped you to understand another person's words and feeling. An *allusion* is a reference to a person, place, writer, or legend—usually, but not always, from an earlier age. To be effective, an allusion must be understood by most people.

In Shakespeare's time, even the common people knew a great deal about mythology and the Bible and ancient history; so, of course, Shakespeare and the other playwrights of his time used many allusions from these areas. You will better enjoy reading *Macbeth* if you are already familiar with the allusions used in the play.

GOLGOTHA: (GOL guh thuh) The Hebrew name for Calvary, the place outside ancient Jerusalem where Christ was crucified.

HECATE: (HECK it) The goddess (or queen) of the witches; she was often represented as having the head of a horse, dog, or boar.

TARQUIN: The last king of Rome, who was so cruel that the Romans rebelled, threw out the monarchy, and installed consuls in place of kings. Among other things, Tarquin ravished (raped) Lucrece as she slept.

NEPTUNE: The Roman god of the sea.

MARK ANTONY: A Roman general supposedly more noble than Octavian Caesar but less powerful. Antony was warm and human. Octavian Caesar was cold, almost emotionless.

BELLONA: The Roman goddess of war, a belligerent lady attended by three handmaids: Blood, Fire, and Famine.

BEELZEBUB: (be ELL zuh bub) A prince of the devils, second only to Satan.

GORGON: (GORE gun) Another name for Medusa, a monster whose hair was a mass of writhing snakes so horrible that anyone seeing the monster was turned to stone.

ACHERON: (ACK uh ron) The "River of Grief," one of the five rivers of hell, or hell itself.

OCTAVIAN CAESAR: (also known as Augustus Caesar) The nephew and heir of Julius Caesar; a Roman general, later a Roman emperor, known for his strength and coldness.

Below are ten quotations from *Macbeth*. Answer the questions that follow each quotation.

1. A messenger from a battlefield announces that Macbeth and Banquo are destroying the enemy. (I,ii,41–45)

> So they
> Doubly redoubled strokes upon the foe:
> Except they meant to bathe in reeking wounds,
> Or memorize another *Golgotha,*
> I cannot tell—

a. What is "Golgotha"?

_____

b. "Reeking" means "steaming," hence the wounds are large and freshly made, the warm blood still "steaming." "Memorize" here means "make memorable" or "make unforgettable." What does this phrase mean: "they meant to . . . memorize another Golgotha"?

_____

_____

54

c. Why (in your opinion) did Shakespeare use this allusion in this speech?

_____

_____

_____

_____

2. A messenger from the battlefield describes Macbeth's fighting against the rebel, the thane of Cawdor. (I,ii,60–64)

> The thane of Cawdor, began a dismal conflict,
> Till that Bellona's bridegroom, lapped in proof,
> Confronted him with self-comparisons,
> Point against point rebellious, arm 'gainst arm,
> Curbing his lavish spirit.

a. Who is "Bellona"?

_____

b. In what sense is Macbeth "Bellona's bridegroom"?

_____

_____

c. Why (in your opinion) did Shakespeare use this allusion?

_____

_____

_____

_____

3. Macbeth is planning to kill King Duncan. He says to himself (II,i,60,63–64):

> . . . and withered murder
> With Tarquin's ravishing strides, toward his design
> Moves like a ghost.

a. Who was "Tarquin"?

_____

b. If murder is progressing "with Tarquin's ravishing strides," exactly HOW is murder moving?

_____

_____

c. Why (in your opinion) did Shakespeare use this allusion?

_____

_____

_____

~~~~~~

4. After he kills King Duncan, Macbeth worries (II,ii,72–73):

> Will all great Neptune's ocean wash this blood
> Clean from my hand?

a. Who was "Neptune"?

_____

b. What is worrying Macbeth in this speech?

_____

_____

c. Why (in your opinion) did Shakespeare use this allusion?

_____

_____

_____

_____

5. After the king has been murdered, the Porter hears a knocking on the castle gate and calls (II,iii,3–4):

> Who's there, in the name of Beelzebub?

a. What or who is "Beelzebub"?

_____

_____

b. Why does the Porter invoke the name of Beelzebub?

_____

_____

c. Why (in your opinion) did Shakespeare use this allusion?

_____

_____

_____

_____

6. Macduff goes to King Duncan and finds him murdered in his sleep. He says to his friends (II,iii,78–79):

> Approach the chamber, and destroy your sight
> With a new Gorgon?

a. What is a "Gorgon"?

_____

_____

b. What does Macduff mean in this speech?

_____

_____

c. Why (in your opinion) did Shakespeare use this allusion?

_____

_____

_____

_____

7. Macbeth, thinking of Banquo, says to himself (III,i,58–61):

> There is none but he
> Whose being I do fear. And under him
> My Genius is rebuked, as it is said
> Mark Antony's was by Caesar.

a. Who is Mark Antony?

_____

b. Who is Caesar?

_____

c. What is Macbeth afraid of?

_____

_____

d. Why (in your opinion) did Shakespeare use this allusion?

_____

_____

_____

_____

8. Macbeth is speaking to Lady Macbeth about his plans for Banquo (III,ii,45–48).

> . . . ere to black Hecate's summons
> The shard-borne beetle with his drowsy hums
> Hath rung night's yawning peal, there shall be done
> A deed of dreadful note.

a. Who is "Hecate"?

_____

b. What is Macbeth really saying?

_____

_____

c. Why (in your opinion) did Shakespeare use this allusion?

_____

_____

_____

_____

9. The witches unexpectedly meet Hecate (III,v,1–9):

> *First Witch*
>   Why, how now, Hecate! you look angerly.
> *Hecate*
>   Have I not reason, beldams as you are,
>   Saucy and overbold? How did you dare
>   To trade and traffic with Macbeth
>   In riddles and affairs of death;
>   And I, the mistress of your charms,
>   The close contriver of all harms,
>   Was never call'd to bear my part,
>   Or show the glory of our art?

a. What is Hecate's mood?

_____

b. Why does Hecate feel as she does about the witches?

_____

_____

10. Hecate adds (III,v,14–16):

>   Get you gone,
>   And at the pit of Acheron
>   Meet me i' the morning.

a. What is "Acheron"?

_____

b. Why does Hecate order the witches to meet her "at the pit of Acheron"?

_____

_____

c. Why (in your opinion) did Shakespeare use this allusion?

_____

_____

_____

_____

21. Similes

Suppose you wanted to say that a particular young actress became a star practically overnight, was spectacular in a couple of roles, and then lost popularity almost as quickly as she had gained it. You might say:

"She shot like Halley's comet across the theater world."

The simile—"Like Halley's comet"—says it all: it stresses the unusual appearance, the brightness, the drama, and the disappearance . . . and it does it in three words that neatly fit into a sentence.

A simile is a comparison that uses "like" or "as."

You already know a great many similes.

light as _____(air)

thin as a _____(rake)

hollow as a _____(drum)

helpless as a _____(babe)

Think of other words to complete the similes. Write your own words in the following unfinished similes.

light as a _____

skinny as a _____

hollow as a _____

helpless as a _____

These are "tired" similes: they have been used so often they have little vitality left. The good writer stretches imagination to create fresh similes that paint thoughtful pictures. The following similes make you think, and think again.

light as the rainbow's leap (Schiller)
thin as a Ritz-Carlton sandwich (Stephen Leacock)
hollow as an actor's laugh (Gelett Burgess)
helpless as an infant caterpillar in a nest of hungry ants (James Montgomery Flagg)

A good writer uses similes:

. . . to make clear some idea or person or place, and
. . . to add drama and color, and
. . . to make the reader think.

Shakespeare's writing is filled with superb similes—and with metaphors, too.

A metaphor is a comparison that does *not* use "like" or "as."

In the hands of a master writer, the metaphor gives sharpness and depth of understanding. It sometimes shocks us into a new awareness. Ray Bradbury wrote of a "windstorm" (breath) from a beast's mouth; Emily Dickinson wrote of the "white assassin" (frost); and T.S. Eliot wrote of the "burnt-out end of smoky days" (twilight).

Someone seeing the young actress and suspecting her popularity will not last might shake a head and say: "Another Halley's comet!" The comparison is not made; it is *implied—suggested.*

> **A simile *makes* a comparison using "like" or "as."**
> **A metaphor *suggests* a comparison.**

1. Below are six excerpts from *Macbeth*. Each is lacking a simile. Check the similes listed below the passages and find exactly the right one to complete each excerpt. Consider first the aptness of each simile to the context, but consider also alliteration and meter.

   a. But signs of nobleness, _____, shall shine
      On all deservers.

   b. Your face, my thane, is _____ where men
      May read strange matters.

   c. And his great love, sharp _____, hath holp him
      To his home before us.

   d.   . . . his virtues

      Will plead _____ against
      The deep damnation of his taking-off;

   e. A heavy summons lies _____ upon me,
      And yet I would not sleep.

   f.   . . . now does he feel his title

      Hang loose upon him, _____
      Upon a dwarfish thief.

      SIMILES:
      like angels trumpet-tongued   like stars
      like a giant's robe   as a book
      like lead   as his spur

2. In column I below are five metaphors. In column II are five definitions. Consider each definition carefully and decide which metaphor it best describes.

I	II
golden round	cowardly fool
cream-fac'd loon	starless night
serpent and worm	extinguishing of a life
"Their candles are all out."	crown
"Out, out, brief candle!"	enemy and son

Finally, examine once again the six similes and the five metaphors you have just read. Select *one* you consider especially effective and explain *why* it is effective. (This exercise should help you to see the importance of metaphorical writing and to become more sensitive to Shakespeare's use of this writing technique.)

_____

_____

_____

22. Imagery

An IMAGE is "the little word-picture used by a poet or prose writer to illustrate, to illuminate and embellish his thought."* The key word is WORD-PICTURE.

All writers use IMAGERY; Shakespeare used it constantly. For one thing, his theater demanded it.

Plays were most often performed in the afternoon. The theater was open; therefore, light. A messenger carrying a torch helped the audience to *see* darkness where darkness did not exist. A word-picture could do the same thing. In the court of Macbeth's castle, where Banquo and his son Fleance are walking, Banquo notes:

> There's husbandry in heaven,
> Their candles are all out.

("Husbandry," remember, means "thrift." See page 13.) Immediately the audience knows—and *feels*—not only that it is night but that it is a starless night . . . a dark night suitable for dark deeds. Such is the magic of IMAGERY.

IMAGERY includes similes and metaphors, but it goes beyond these. It includes any kind of word-picture.

In *Macbeth,* Shakespeare used all kinds of images, but some he used again and again. These recurring images help us to *see* a character in a certain way; through repetition, they also help us to form a mental image of that character that goes far beyond the physical image.

1. One recurring image deals with CLOTHING.

If you see an eight-year-old boy wearing a T-shirt so big it falls to his knees, what are you likely to conclude? (That he borrowed the shirt from his father or big brother) What additional idea will almost immediately follow? (That the boy wants to be like his father or brother; that he yearns to be a man before his time) If the boy starts to climb a tree or to play ball, what will happen? (The too-large clothing will hamper

*Definition by Caroline Spurgeon in *Shakespeare's Imagery, and What It Tells Us* (New York: Cambridge University Press, 1952)

him . . . trip him up . . . get in his way. It doesn't *fit,* and so it looks silly and makes the boy act in a silly fashion.)

Early in *Macbeth* (I,iii, 112–113) when a messenger addresses Macbeth as "thane of Cawdor," Macbeth retorts:

> The thane of Cawdor lives: why do you dress me
> In borrow'd robes?

With this question, the clothing imagery is launched. It is strengthened, almost immediately, when Banquo says thoughtfully:

> New honors come upon him,
> Like our strange garments, cleave not to their mold
> But with the aid of use.

You should have little difficulty with this image. Most teenagers hate new jeans until they have been worn enough to "cleave" to the mold—to fit perfectly. Almost any new garment feels strange, at first, until it becomes truly "ours."

Here are some additional CLOTHING images.

(II,iv, 49) When Macduff hears that Macbeth is going to Scone to be crowned, he hopes all will go well, but fears, "Lest our old robes sit easier than our new!"

(V,ii, 17–18) In the final battle when everything is turning against Macbeth, one nobleman says sorrowfully:

> He (Macbeth) cannot buckle his distemper'd cause
> Within the belt of rule.

(V,ii, 23–25) Another noble adds:

> . . . now does he feel his title
> Hang loose about him, like a giant's robe
> Upon a dwarfish thief.

Think about and discuss the three CLOTHING images above. In each case try to *see* the image Shakespeare was creating. Then answer the following questions.

a. What do all the CLOTHING images have in common? What picture do they convey?

_____

_____

_____

_____

b. How do these CLOTHING images affect our picture of Macbeth?

_____

_____

c. How do these CLOTHING images relate to Macbeth's killing of Duncan? To his having himself crowned King of Scotland?

_____

_____

_____

_____

_____

2. A second recurring image deals with BLOOD. Throughout the play, Shakespeare uses "blood" or "bloody", "bleed" or "bleeding" more than forty times. The image first appears in I,ii, when Duncan, meeting a bleeding sergeant, asks: "What bloody man is this?" The play has barely opened, yet already we are steeped in blood. A few lines later the sergeant describes Macbeth as wielding a sword "which smok'd with bloody execution." When Lady Macbeth thinks ahead to the killing of Duncan (I,v), she calls on the spirits to "make thick my blood."

On and on the images run, almost colliding in their frequency. We hear of BLOODY knives (obvious) and of a BLOODY piece of work—but also of BLOODY-sceptered, of a BLOODY stage, even of BLOODY INSTRUCTIONS.

Here are a few BLOOD images.

(II,ii, 72–74) Macbeth, after killing Duncan, cries:

> Will all great Neptune's ocean wash this blood
> Clean from my hand? No; this my hand will rather
> The multitudinous seas incarnadine,*
> Making the green one red.
> (*incarnadine: redden)

(III,iv, 159–161) Macbeth, after several murders, says to his wife:

> . . . I am in blood
> Steep'd in so far that, should I wade no more,
> Returning were as tedious as go o'er.

(III,vi, 34–36) A noble, musing on what has been happening in Scotland, prays that, with God's help:

> . . . we may again
> Give to our tables meat, sleep to our nights,
> Free from our feasts and banquets bloody knives . . .

(V,i, 46–47) Lady Macbeth, in a sleepwalking scene, cries:

> Here's the smell of the blood still: all the perfumes of
> Arabia will not sweeten this little hand.

Think about and discuss the four BLOOD images above. In each case try to *see* the image Shakespeare was creating. Then answer the following questions.

a. Why is the BLOOD imagery especially appropriate for the play, *Macbeth?*

_____

_____

_____

b. How does the BLOOD imagery affect the way we see Macbeth as a person?

_____

_____

_____

When you read *Macbeth,* be alert—not only for images related to CLOTHING and to BLOOD, but also for images related to:

> DARKNESS and LIGHT
> DISEASE
> PREDATORY ANIMALS
> SLEEP
> SPEED (riding, striding, etc.)

You will find that the imagery is responsible for much of our emotional involvement in the play. As our heads absorb the ideas, our hearts absorb the images—until we understand Macbeth as well, or as little, as we understand a member of our family.

Structure

23. Structure

What is a TRAGEDY?

A TRAGEDY is a dramatic telling of a serious story in which the leading character is, through his or her own faults, brought to a catastrophe.

Notice the four essential elements:

1. It is dramatic.
2. It is serious.
3. The leading character meets with total defeat.
4. The defeat results from flaws in the leading character.

The above four elements are essential to *any* tragedy, classical or contemporary. But a fifth element should be added for the former: in classical tragedy, the hero or heroine must be superior, in status or in virtue. This is necessary so that the "fall," caused by the hero's tragic flaw, may be a meaningful one.

Consider Shakespeare's plays. In *King Lear,* the hero is a good king who has ruled for a long time. His flaw: he is overly susceptible to flattery. In *Othello,* the hero is a Moor successful in commerce and in love. His flaw: he is insanely jealous. In *Macbeth,* the hero is a respected thane who becomes a king. His flaw: he is ruthlessly ambitious.

(This fifth element—that the hero should be "superior"—is *not* essential in modern tragedies. In *Death of a Salesman* by Arthur Miller, the "hero" is Willie Loman, an ordinary salesman. Willie is in no way a superior being. He wants to be a good salesman and a good husband and father, but he is simply not up to it. His fatal flaw, if it can be called that, is that he wants to be more than he is and he wants his sons to be more than he is. His defeat leaves the audience with a feeling of sadness, of futility, while the defeat of a classical hero (e.g., Macbeth) leaves the audience with a feeling of grief mixed with triumph: grief that so "superior" a person can fall so low, and triumph that good once again has overwhelmed evil.)

Let's consider these five essential elements in an imaginary play, a *classical* tragedy. In each exercise, answer the questions *before* you read the commentary that follows them.

1. Select a leading character. Who would be better: King Thomas of Magic Island or Joe Shmo, a small-town storekeeper? (Surely your answer is—King Thomas.)

    a. In which of the two characters would most people be interested? _____

    b. Which of the two characters would affect a larger number of people? _____

    c. If they are to meet with total defeat, which of the two would "fall" the far-thest? _____

    (Now you should understand why the leading character should be a superior individual: superior in status or in virtue.)

2. Select one of the following plot lines.

    a. King Thomas has a toothache. He seeks a dentist who will help him without hurting him.

    b. The people of Aroo, a neighboring island, ask King Thomas to help them against the tyrant Bobo. King Thomas and his troops go to their aid.

    Which did you choose? _____

    The second, of course, for the action must be SERIOUS. The first plot line might do for a comedy, but never for a tragedy. It simply isn't important enough; it doesn't af-fect anyone except the owner of the tooth.

3. Select a possible ending for the play.

    a. King Thomas, after saving the people of Aroo from the tyrant Bobo, decides to rule the island himself rather than give it back to the inhabitants. By accident, someone drops a box of shrimp on his foot which gets infected, causing his death.

    b. King Thomas, after saving the people of Aroo from the tyrant Bobo, decides to rule the island himself rather than give it back to the inhabitants. A few of the natives kill him.

    Which did you choose? _____

    King Thomas dies in both versions, but in the first version, he dies in a silly way. His death has no real meaning; it is an accident. In the second version, his death is the re-sult of his actions, directly related to his deeds. So the second version would be more satisfying and more meaningful.

4. Select a *reason* for the decision or action that leads to the ending of the play.

    a. King Thomas, halfway through the play, has conquered Bobo, the tyrant. He remembers his father, King Leonard, who once ruled both Magic and Aroo, and he craves the greater power and wealth that will be his if he, too, rules both islands. He refuses to return the island to the inhabitants and becomes a tyrant himself. They kill him.

    b. King Thomas, halfway through the play, has conquered Bobo, the tyrant. He wants to return the island to the inhabitants, but they are fighting among themselves, so he sets himself up as a temporary ruler to bring peace. Some of the inhabitants kill him.

    Which did you choose? _____

The effect of King Thomas's decision is the same in both versions: his takeover of Aroo; but his *motive* makes a difference. In the second version, he takes over for a good reason: to help the people, to bring them peace. His killing would be wrong. It would offend us and would be, in a sense, unfair. In the first version, he takes over for a selfish reason: to acquire greater power and wealth for himself. In this situation his killing seems inevitable, even right. It is the direct result of a flaw (too much ambition) in *his* character. He has made his bed, and now he must lie (or die) in it.

5. Select a method for presenting King Thomas's story.
   a. The playwright, through the king's friend, tells the story of the battle between the king and Bobo.
   b. The playwright develops a scene in which the battle actually takes place on stage, culminating in a duel between the king and Bobo. The king is victorious, Bobo slain.

Which did you choose? _____

The first method would give us all the facts, but we would never feel truly involved. The second method would involve us immediately and directly. We would quickly find ourselves cheering on the king and hoping for the demise of Bobo. The second method is dramatic; the first is not. Rule 1 for drama: show, don't tell.

The FIVE essential elements of a classical tragedy:
1. That the leading character be superior (in status or in virtue)
2. That the action be serious
3. That the ending be catastrophic and fitting
4. That the catastrophic ending be the result of a flaw in the hero or heroine
5. That the presentation be dramatic.

When you think of the structure of a tragedy, think of a pyramid.

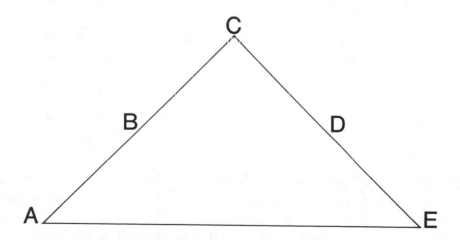

The action begins at A, increases steadily through B, reaching a peak at C. It then decreases through D, coming to defeat at E. C is the *point of no return*; in Shakespearian plays, it usually occurs in Act III. It is the moment when the leading character cannot turn back; he is committed to a certain course of action. It is the moment when success is in his hands, yet defeat is already present, peering from behind a curtain or from around a corner.

In *Macbeth:*

A. The play starts with witches and thunder and lightning, all suggesting the horrors to come. The second scene tells us of the battle that just took place, emphasizes the violence of the era, and praises Macbeth's courage. (The play is well begun. Macbeth, a good man and a brave one, wins the applause of all; yet we are edgy about what is to come.)

B. The rest of Act I and all of Act II show Macbeth in action. He plans a murder; he commits a murder; he begins to dread what he has done. He has himself crowned King of Scotland. To secure his position, he orders more murders.

C. He *is* the king. He has the power he sought. But at a banquet, Banquo's ghost rules in bloody splendor. Macbeth, shaken, muses: "It will have blood. They say blood will have blood." At this point, he *knows* that he will reap the crop he has sowed. He forces himself to go on, but we soon hear that Duncan's sons are gathering an army to bring against Macbeth. *This* is the point of no return. *This* is the peak. As Macbeth reaches the top, he has also reached (and he's intelligent enough to suspect this) the time for a descent.

D. Macbeth goes to the witches—and believes their prophecies because he wants to believe them. He has been told to fear Macduff, so, unable to reach Macduff himself, he has Macduff's wife and children killed—a stupid action, an illustration of "blood will have blood." Lady Macbeth is overwhelmed with the horrors she helped to initiate. The forces are gathering under Malcolm and Macduff.

E. Macbeth has a doctor summoned to treat his wife—and wishes he could find a doctor to heal his country's ills. Yet he knows there is no miracle cure for either. The witches' prophecies turn out to be equivocal: not what they seemed. Macbeth feels betrayed—alone—but he has physical courage still as he faces Macduff in single combat. The end is foreordained: Macbeth is killed. The usurper is dead, as a result of his own actions; and the rightful heir is restored to the throne.

There you have it. When you think of the action in a TRAGEDY, think of climbing a mountain until you reach the peak (C), and then think of the rapid but dangerous descent.

One word more: a TRAGEDY is basically a conflict between good and evil. The leading character may be good in the beginning and then become evil (as in *Macbeth*); may be evil throughout (as in *Richard III*); or may be good throughout (as in *King Lear*.) But good or evil, the leading character has a "tragic flaw" which leads to his destruction. And always: good triumphs.

FOR DISCUSSION

1. What important leaders of the 20th century might well be the subject of a tragedy? Why?

2. Is real life like a tragedy? Consider Hitler's rise: his desire to help the Germans weakened in World War I; his rise to power; his mastery of much of Europe (his peak); his wanton destruction of the Jews and defeated peoples; his decline; his death. Analyze the lives of other leaders in the same fashion.

3. Since classical times, it has been believed that one purpose of tragedy is to purge the emotions: to permit us to take part in a glorious enterprise, to fall into evil, and to face the catastrophe that follows the fall. As we leave the theater, we feel purged, cleansed. We have been touched by evil, but have also been freed from it. We feel uplifted, ready for new beginnings. Consider this theory in relation to any tragedies you have read. Consider it in relation to 20th-century wars.

4. The word "tragedy" is used carelessly today. Is an earthquake a tragedy? Is the haphazard killing of a dozen people by a maniac a tragedy? Is the death of several small children in a burning house a tragedy? Why, or why not?

24. Characterization

What do we know about Macbeth?

> He's about forty years old.
> He's a Scottish noble and a general.
> He's married to Lady Macbeth.

That's the historical data. When you know that, how well do you know Macbeth? Not at all well. Facts are useful, but they seldom help us to a true understanding of a person.

In a Shakespearian play—indeed, in most plays—few facts are given directly. Instead, as in *Macbeth,* you slowly develop an understanding of a character. As you watch Macbeth's actions, listen to his words, notice his reactions to the deeds of others, you begin to *know* Macbeth in a very real way.

Consider each of the following passages carefully. (All are from Act I.) Then answer the questions that follow each passage.

1. Macbeth faces the rebel Macdonwald on the battlefield. The sergeant reports:

> For brave Macbeth—well he deserves that name—
> Disdaining fortune, with his brandish'd steel
> . . . unseam'd him from the nave to the chaps,
> And fix'd his head upon our battlements.
> (I,ii, 18–19, 24–25)

What does this report tell us about Macbeth?

_____

_____

2. When the witches prophesy that Macbeth is the thane of Glamis, will be thane of
   Cawdor, and "king hereafter," Banquo (who is with Macbeth) says:

   > Good sir, why do you start, and seem to fear
   > Things that do sound so fair? (I,iii, 52–53)

   a. How does Macbeth react to the prophecies?

   _____

   _____

   b. What does this suggest about Macbeth's character?

   _____

   _____

3. Macbeth is already thane of Glamis. When he is named thane of Cawdor, he mutters:

   > Glamis, and thane of Cawdor:
   > The greatest is behind. (I, iii, 122–123)

   ("Behind" here means "still ahead.")
   What already is in Macbeth's mind?

   _____

4. King Duncan announces that he is naming his son Malcolm as Prince of Cumberland—that is, his heir. Macbeth says, in an aside:

   > The Prince of Cumberland! that is a step
   > On which I must fall down, or else o'erleap,
   > For in my way it lies. (I, iv, 55–57)

   a. How does Macbeth react to the news that Duncan has named his elder son his heir?

   _____

   b. How do Macbeth's words indicate what is in his mind?

   _____

   _____

5. Lady Macbeth receives a letter from her husband telling about the witches' prophecies. She muses:

   > Glamis thou art, and Cawdor, and shalt be
   > What thou art promis'd: yet do I fear thy nature;
   > It is too full o' the milk of human kindness
   > To catch the nearest way. (I, v, 15–18)

a. What does this passage tell us about Lady Macbeth?

_____

_____

b. What additional information does it give us about Macbeth?

_____

_____

6. While Macbeth is thinking about the elimination of the king, he thinks:

> . . . that we but teach
> Bloody instructions, which being taught return
> To plague the inventor: (I, vii, 8–10)

a. What is in Macbeth's mind? What is he probably planning to do?

_____

_____

b. What else does this passage tell us about Macbeth's character?

_____

_____

7. As they are talking about the murder of Duncan, Lady Macbeth says to her husband:

> Art thou afeard
> To be the same in thine own act and valor
> As thou art in desire? (I, vii, 42–44)

a. What does this passage suggest about Lady Macbeth's character?

_____

_____

b. What additional information does it give us about Macbeth?

_____

_____

8. Lady Macbeth pleads violently for her husband to be a "man"—to kill the king and become king. When she finishes an impassioned speech, Macbeth asks briefly:

> If we should fail? (I, vii, 65)

a. Lady Macbeth is urging her husband to kill the king. What is Macbeth's reaction?

_____

_____

b. What does his reaction tell us about Macbeth?

_____

_____

9. They come to a decision: Duncan is doomed. Macbeth ends the scene with these words:

> False face must hide what the false heart doth know. (I,vii,92)

What additional information about Macbeth do we learn from this passage?

_____

_____

_____

Reread the nine passages and your analysis of each. What do you know about Macbeth _now?_ List his qualities, his character traits. Notice that you know all this through his reactions (to the witches' prophecies, to his wife's urging, to the act of murder itself) and through the reactions of others (of Banquo, of Lady Macbeth).

_____

_____

_____

_____

_____

_____

_____

_____

_____

_____

As the play develops, so also will develop your knowledge of Macbeth—of how he thinks, of what he believes, of his innermost being.

In the same way, you will learn a great deal about Lady Macbeth, and, to a lesser extent, about Banquo, Macduff, and the other characters.

By the time you have finished the play, you will _know_ these characters well, because Shakespeare showed you—_showed_ you, not _told_ you. This is part of Shakespeare's greatness: his ability to depict a character in its complexity, to help us to gain deep insights into that character, and to involve us emotionally in the character's plight.

FOR DISCUSSION

After you have read the play, you may wish to consider the following questions. (There are few "right" answers. Even the experts differ.)

1. Would Macbeth have murdered Duncan if Lady Macbeth had not encouraged him?

2. Is Lady Macbeth inhuman, as some critics insist? Is she possessed by evil spirits?

3. Banquo suspects Macbeth all through Acts I and II. Why didn't he flee as Malcolm did? What does this tell us about Banquo's character?

4. Macduff also suspected Macbeth and almost immediately left the court. Soon he left Scotland as well. But he left behind his wife and children. What does this tell us about Macduff's character?

25. Dialog

DIALOG: a conversation between two or more people.

Example:

> STACY: "Let's go to the mall."
> PAUL: "Good idea. Want a pizza?"
> STACY: "You bet!"

Any conversation, no matter how brief, how ordinary, how inane, is DIALOG. A play, by its nature, is 100% dialog. And that raises some interesting questions.

1. How does the playwright tell you where the action is taking place?

2. How does the playwright tell you what is happening?

3. How does the playwright tell you who is involved and what they are like?

4. How does the playwright tell you about the weather, or about something that happened in the past, or about how the characters feel?

ANSWER: through DIALOG.

In addition, in Elizabethan times, playwrights had three additional problems:

1. Little scenery was used. Without expensive sets, how did a playwright convey a picture of the locale where the action is taking place?

2. Artificial lighting did not exist, and performances always took place during the day. How did the playwright indicate that it was a dark night or a moonlit night, or that it was a cloudy day?

3. Women were not permitted on stage. Boys played the female roles. With this in mind, how did a playwright make love scenes realistic—and romantic?

ANSWER: through DIALOG.

This means DIALOG is absolutely critical. Frequently, a brief bit of dialog will fulfill several purposes at one time.

Consider the beginning of Act II, Scene i. Banquo enters the court of Macbeth's castle. His son, Fleance, bearing a torch, precedes him.

> BANQUO: How goes the night, boy?
> FLEANCE: The moon is down; I have not heard the clock.
> BANQUO: And she goes down at twelve.
> FLEANCE: I take 't, 'tis later, sir.

Let's see what Shakespeare tells us in these four short lines.

1. It is night.

2. The moon is down, so it is a *dark* night.

3. It is after midnight.

4. The relationship between Banquo and Fleance is comfortable, even affectionate (the casual concern in Banquo's addressing his son as "boy"; the quiet respect in Fleance's addressing his father as "sir").

The scene continues with a longer speech by Banquo.

> Hold, take my sword. There's husbandry in heaven,
> Their candles are all out. Take thee that too.
> A heavy summons lies like lead upon me,
> And yet I would not sleep. Merciful powers,
> Restrain in me the cursed thoughts that nature
> Gives way to in repose!

What does Shakespeare tell us in this single speech?

5. Banquo feels fairly safe at the moment or he wouldn't relinquish his sword to his young son.

6. The night is *very* dark. In addition to there being no moon, there are no stars. This emphasis on darkness makes us wary and suspicious.

7. Banquo says, "Take thee that, too" and "that" must refer to his buckler, a small shield. Banquo seems to be shedding his defenses.

8. Banquo is very tired ("a heavy summons lies . . . upon me") yet he doesn't wish to sleep. ("Summons," here, means a *call* to sleep, or extreme tiredness.) Why doesn't he? Because he fears the "cursed thoughts" that might come when he begins to relax.

9. Remember that Banquo heard the witches' prophecies to Macbeth, and he witnessed Macbeth's reactions. His "cursed thoughts" are surely related to these prophecies. Does he fear what Macbeth will do? Probably not, not yet. He is—uneasy. He senses that something is wrong. Both the darkness of the night and his own frightening thoughts confirm this.

Look at the next few lines. Macbeth and a servant with a torch enter.

> BANQUO: Give me my sword.
>   Who's there?
> MACBETH: A friend.
> BANQUO: What, sir, not yet at rest? The king's a-bed.

What more do we learn?

10. Apparently the torch does not at once identify the person who entered. Banquo's first

reaction is to call for his sword. Instinctively he feels the need for a means of defense, even though he is within the courtyard of Macbeth's castle.

11. Macbeth's brief answer ("A friend") seems simple enough. Yet in this charged uneasy atmosphere, it questions itself: Is Macbeth a friend to Banquo?

12. Banquo's response is odd. He and his son are in the courtyard of Macbeth's castle. Yet he questions at once why Macbeth is there, why he hasn't retired. Does he suspect that Macbeth's thoughts are "heavy" too? That Macbeth is full of plans, plans that are not pleasant?

13. Banquo gives himself away when he notes: "The king's a-bed." Involuntarily, he links Macbeth and the king, and at the same time emphasizes Macbeth's restlessness and Duncan's vulnerability. (We are, after all, most vulnerable when we are asleep.)

Be aware of what Shakespeare has done. In these fourteen lines of dialog (very "ordinary" dialog), he has:

> Provided a setting
> Contributed to our knowledge of Banquo's character
> Created an atmosphere of tension, almost of anticipation
> Placed Banquo and Macbeth, just for a moment, in opposition.

You try it.

Lady Macbeth went up to murder Duncan, but comes down with the deed undone. "Had he not resembled/ My father as he slept, I had done 't." So Macbeth goes up to do the killing. Below is the dialog between husband and wife immediately after the murder. (II,ii,16–27)

MACBETH: I have done the deed. Didst thou not hear a noise?
LADY MACBETH: I heard the owl scream and the crickets cry.
    Did not you speak?
MACBETH: When?
LADY M.:   Now.
MACBETH: As I descended?
LADY M.: Aye.
MACBETH: Hark!
    Who lies in the second chamber?
LADY M.:   Donalbain.
MACBETH: (looking on his hands)
    This is a sorry sight.
LADY M.: A foolish thought, to say a sorry sight.

1. Macbeth calmly announces he has "done the deed," he has murdered his king. Immediately he asks: "Didst thou not hear a noise?" What does this bit of dialog tell us?

_____

_____

2. Lady Macbeth's answer is in two parts. What do we learn about her from the first part: "I heard the owl scream and the crickets cry"? (See reference to owls, page 19.) Her *first* statement is as matter-of-fact as Macbeth's *first* statement. But she immediately adds: "Did you not speak?" Is Lady Macbeth as calm about this murder as she pretends? What do the words, "Did you not speak?" tell us about her?

_____

_____

_____

_____

3. What is the overall effect of the short lines from Macbeth's "When?" to Lady Macbeth's "Donalbain"?

_____

_____

4. What's happening inside Macbeth when he says: "This is a sorry sight"?

_____

_____

5. What does Lady Macbeth mean when she answers him?

_____

_____

6. Which is the stronger: Macbeth or Lady Macbeth? Why?

_____

_____

7. Do you think Macbeth will suffer from remorse or from conscience in the future? Why, or why not?

_____

_____

8. Do you think Lady Macbeth will suffer from remorse or from conscience in the future? Why, or why not?

_____

_____

Now list all the information you received in these lines of dialog.

_____

_____

_____

_____
_____
_____
_____
_____
_____
_____

You see? Shakespeare packed an incredible amount of information into this short exchange between two characters. He advanced your knowledge of the plot and your understanding of Macbeth and Lady Macbeth. He made you wonder how these two would handle themselves in the future, how they would handle their guilt. Amazing, isn't it?

Do you have to analyze each group of speeches as you read the play? Of course not. Your subconscious mind will do much of the work for you, but you should be aware of the dialog, of its importance and its power. It will enhance your overall enjoyment.

26. Foreshadowing

Have you ever stood alone in an open place and suddenly become conscious of a giant shadow looming above you?

Have you ever been on a picnic on a sunny day and found yourself unexpectedly in the shade?

The shadow may have signaled the approach of your brother; the shade may have signaled the coming of a thunderstorm.

FORESHADOWING indicates—hints at, suggests—what is coming. It is a *signal* pointing to a future event.

The good writer rarely allows an event to happen without first providing FORESHADOWING.

FORESHADOWING comes in all "sizes and shapes." Some examples:

> A man leaves his home one day when the roads are icy. "Don't worry about me!" he brags. "I've been driving for twenty years without a single accident!" Backing out of the driveway, he loses control of the car, and skids into a passing police van. (A boasting speech may foreshadow a coming disaster.)

> A woman awakens on the morning of her bar exam, a test that lawyer candidates must pass. She looks outside: it's a dark day, and it's raining hard. She shivers. She fails the test. (Weather may foreshadow defeat.)

> A fifteen-year-old is cycling down Main Street when a black cat crosses in front of him. Ten minutes later his brakes won't work and he slams into a brick wall. (A superstition may foreshadow an accident.)

Shakespeare is a master of FORESHADOWING and, in *Macbeth*, he uses it frequently and with telling effect.

Act I, Scene i opens in "a desert place" (arid, sterile, empty). Thunder roars; lightning flashes (violence). Three witches enter (devilish work afoot). Before the first word is spoken, we shiver; we *know* we are in the presence of evil. The violence signals the murders that are to come; the devilish work signals the evil that is behind the murders; the sterility signals the barrenness of murder, of any evil. What a powerful beginning, thanks to skillful foreshadowing!

Act I, Scene iii. The witches greet Macbeth with their prophecies.

> hail to thee, thane of Glamis!
> hail to thee, thane of Cawdor!
> thou shalt be king hereafter!

Their prophecies plant the seed of ambition (or foster one already there) and foreshadow the single, most influential scene in the play: the murder of King Duncan.

YOUR TURN

Read each of the following passages; then answer the questions.

1. After the witches disappear, Macbeth wishes they had stayed, but Banquo says:

> Were such things here as we do speak about?
> Or have we eaten on the insane root
> That takes the reason prisoner? (I,iii,84–86)

a. Paraphrase Banquo's speech.

_____

_____

_____

b. What might it foreshadow?

_____

_____

2. Later King Duncan, hearing about Cawdor's rebellion and treason, says:

> There's no art
> To find the mind's construction in the face:
> He was a gentleman on whom I built
> An absolute trust. (I,iv,13–16)

Immediately afterward, Macbeth enters and Duncan greets him:

> O worthiest cousin!

a. What is Duncan's chief lament?

_____

_____

b. What does his speech combined with his greeting to Macbeth foreshadow?

_____

_____

3. As Duncan approaches Macbeth's castle for a visit, Lady Macbeth says:

> The raven himself is hoarse
> That croaks the fatal entrance of Duncan
> Under my battlements. (I,v,42–44)

a. Why does Lady Macbeth refer to a raven? (See page 19.)

_____

_____

b. What does this speech clearly foreshadow?

_____

_____

4. Immediately after the murder, Macbeth hears a voice:

> Still it cried "Sleep no more!" to all the house:
> "Glamis hath murder'd sleep, and therefore Cawdor
> Shall sleep no more: Macbeth shall sleep no more." (II,ii,50–52)

a. What does this speech foreshadow?

_____

_____

b. How does it deepen our knowledge of Macbeth's character?

_____

_____

5. After the king has been murdered but while the deed is known only to Macbeth and Lady Macbeth, Macduff and Lennox visit Macbeth's home. Lennox describes the night that has just passed.

> The night has been unruly: where we lay,
> Our chimneys were blown down, and, as they say,
> Lamentings heard i' the air, strange screams of death,
> And prophesying with accents terrible
> Of dire combustion and confus'd events
> New hatch'd to the woeful time: the obscure bird
> Clamor'd the livelong night: some say, the earth
> Was feverous and did shake. (II,iii,58–65)

a. What happened during the night that amazed and horrified Lennox? (The obscure bird is the night owl.)

_____

_____

_____

_____

b. How does this foreshadow something else that happened the same night?

_____

_____

c. How do the happenings of the night "fit in" with the Elizabethan theory concerning the Order of the Universe? (See page 46.)

_____

_____

_____

In the future, as you read a story or watch a TV movie, be alert for examples of FORESHADOWING. This awareness can sharpen your emotional involvement in a work, and therefore sharpen your understanding and enjoyment.

As you read *Macbeth,* keep your eyes and mind open, and you will find that Shakespeare has provided all kinds of signs and signals and warnings to help you on the journey through this fascinating play.

UNIT VI

Analysis of Key Scenes

27. The Witches' Prophecies
Act I, Scene iii

Imagine this scene. The three witches have gathered on the heath and are huddled around a cauldron. Macbeth and Banquo, returning from the battlefield, enter and see the witches. Now read the passage below.

MACBETH: So foul and fair a day I have not seen.	1
BANQUO: How far is't call'd to Forres? What are these	2
So wither'd, and so wild in their attire,	3
That look not like th' inhabitants o' the earth,	4
And yet are on 't? Live you? or are you aught	5
That man may question? You seem to understand me,	6
By each at once her choppy finger laying	7
Upon her skinny lips: you should be women,	8
And yet your beards forbid me to interpret	9
That you are so.	10

1. Turn to the sketch of the Globe Playhouse on page 35. Where are the witches probably standing? How did you arrive at your answer?

_____

_____

_____

2. Where (possibly) do Macbeth and Banquo enter?

_____

_____

3. (Line 1) What does Macbeth mean by this apparent contradiction? (Think. If you need help, see page 38.)

_____

_____

4. (Lines 2–10) Describe the witches, using this speech of Banquo's as your source.

_____

_____

_____

_____

_____

5. Find *two* examples of alliteration. (See page 48.)

_____

_____

6. Imagine this scene again. See the three witches (from Banquo's description). See Macbeth and Banquo to one side. Is your picture vivid?

_____

7. Review iambic pentameter (see page 51). Read the passage aloud, stressing the second syllable of each foot. Notice there are many variations; the meter is *not* rigid.

> How fár/ is't cáll'd/ to Fór/ res? Whát/ are thése/
> So wíth/ er'd, ańd/ so wíld/ in theír/ attíre,/
> That loók/ not líke/ th' ínháb/ itants óf/ the eárth,/
> And yét/ are ón ' t?/ Live yóu?/ or afe/ you aúght/
> That mań/ may queś/ tion? You seém/ to uń/ derstánd me,/
> By eaćh/ at ónce/ her chóp/ py fiń/ ger laýing/
> Upoń/ her skín/ ny lipś:/ you shoúld/ be wómen,/
> And yét/ your beárds/ forbíd/ me tó/ intefpret/
> That yóu/ are só./

8. Now read the passage again, but this time let the iambic flow naturally so that you can still hear the stressed syllables, but barely. This time concentrate on the meaning of the words. Are you beginning to get the *flavor* of Shakespeare's writing?

Fine. Go on to Chapter 28.

28. The Witches' Prophecies (continued)
Act I, Scene iii

In the last chapter you developed a sharp, vivid picture of the three witches and of Macbeth and Banquo standing to one side. The scene continues. Read the section below.

MACBETH:	Speak, if you can: what are you?	11
FIRST WITCH:	All hail, Macbeth! hail to thee, thane of Glamis!	12
SECOND WITCH:	All hail, Macbeth! hail to thee, thane of Cawdor!	13
THIRD WITCH:	All hail, Macbeth, thou shalt be king hereafter!	14
BANQUO:	Good sir, why do you start, and seem to fear	15

Things that do sound so fair? I' the name of truth,	16
Are ye fantastical, or that indeed	17
Which outwardly ye show? My noble partner	18
You greet with present grace and great prediction	19
Of noble having and of royal hope,	20
That he seems rapt withal: to me you speak not:	21
If you can look into the seeds of time,	22
And say which grain will grow and which will not,	23
Speak then to me, who neither beg nor fear	24
Your favors nor your hate.	25
FIRST WITCH: Hail!	26
SECOND WITCH: Hail!	27
THIRD WITCH: Hail!	28
FIRST WITCH: Lesser than Macbeth, and greater.	29
SECOND WITCH: Not so happy, yet much happier.	30
THIRD WITCH: Thou shalt get (beget) kings, though thou be none;	31
So all hail, Macbeth and Banquo!	32
FIRST WITCH: Banquo and Macbeth, all hail!	33

1. There seem to be three prophecies for Macbeth, but there are really only two. Macbeth is already thane of Glamis. According to the witches, what two other positions will he attain?

_____

_____

2. According to Banquo (lines 15 and 16) how does Macbeth react to the prophecies? Is this a normal reaction? How would *you* react if someone predicted you would be President one day?

_____

_____

_____

3. What favor does Banquo ask of the three witches?

_____

_____

4. Look at the three prophecies pertaining to Banquo (lines 29–32). Then study the "family tree" of Scottish kings on page 8. Did the prophecies to Banquo come true? Explain your answer. ("Get" means "beget"; that is, to father, to produce offspring.)

_____

_____

_____

_____

_____

_____

5. According to Banquo, how does Macbeth receive the news that he will be King of Scotland? Is there anything suspicious about this reaction?

_____

_____

6. Find an example of alliteration (see page 48) in Banquo's speech.

_____

7. Which character, Macbeth or Banquo, seems more stunned by the witches' prophecies? Suggest a possible reason for this.

_____

_____

8. Based on Macbeth's reaction and Banquo's reaction to the prophecies, of which should the present king be more wary?

_____

9. Review iambic pentameter (see page 51). Read the passage aloud, stressing the second syllable of each foot.

> Good sír,/ why dó/ you stárt,/ and séem/ to feár/
> Things thát/ do soúnd/ so faír?/ I' the náme/ of trúth,/
> Are yé/ fantás/ ticál,/ or thát/ indeéd/
> Which óut/ wardlý/ ye shów?/ My nó/ ble páftner/
> You gréet/ with prés/ ent gráce/ and gréat/ predíction/
> Of nó/ ble háv/ ing ańd/ of róy/ al hópe,/
> That hé/ seems rápt/ withál:/ to mé/ you speák not:/
> If yóu/ can loók/ intó/ the seéds/ of tíme,/
> And sáy/ which gráin/ will grów/ and whích/ will nót,/
> Speak thén/ to mé,/ who neí/ ther beǵ/ nor feár/
> Your fá/ vors nór/ your háte./

10. Now read the passage again, but this time let the iambic flow naturally so that you can still hear the stressed syllables, but barely. Concentrate on the meaning of the words.

Before going on, read aloud once more the excerpts from *Macbeth* given in Chapters 27 and 28. If possible, have different people take different roles.

> Can you feel the iambic pentameter rhythm?
> Can you sense the tension between the witches and Macbeth?
> Can you see the beginning of tension between Macbeth and Banquo?

Time now to go on to Chapter 29.

29. The Witches' Prophecies (continued)

Act I, Scene iii

In the preceding two chapters you "saw" the witches and "heard" their prophecies to Macbeth and Banquo. Read the section below.

MACBETH: Stay, you imperfect speakers, tell me more:	34
By Sinel's death I know I am thane of Glamis;	35
But how of Cawdor? the thane of Cawdor lives,	36
A prosperous gentleman; and to be king	37
Stands not within the prospect of belief,	38
No more than to be Cawdor. Say from whence	39
You owe this strange intelligence? or why	40
Upon this blasted heath you stop our way	41
With such prophetic greeting? Speak, I charge you.	42
[Witches vanish.]	
BANQUO: The earth hath bubbles as the water has,	43
And these are of them: whither are they vanish'd?	44
MACBETH: Into the air, and what seem'd corporal melted	45
As breath into the wind. Would they had stay'd!	46
BANQUO: Were such things here as we do speak about?	47
Or have we eaten on the insane root	48
That takes the reason prisoner?	49
MACBETH: Your children shall be kings.	50
BANQUO: You shall be king.	50
MACBETH: And thane of Cawdor too: went it not so?	51
BANQUO: To the selfsame tune and words.	52

1. Which of the men, Macbeth or Banquo, is more excited by the prophecies? How do you know?

2. What does Macbeth say about the possibility of his becoming king?

3. The witches vanish (line 42). Look at the sketch of the Globe Playhouse (page 35) and ask yourself: "*How* did the witches vanish? *How* did the cauldron disappear?"

4. Study lines 45 and 46, and lines 47, 48, and 49. Describe the difference between the way the two men are reacting to the witches' prophecies. What does this tell us about each of them?

_____

_____

_____

_____

5. Find a simile in lines 45 and 46. In your opinion _why_ did Shakespeare use this simile? What is he suggesting? (Corporal: having bodily substance; something one can see and touch.)

_____

_____

_____

6. Read the excerpt on page 85 once again. This time, "mouth" it—that is, form each syllable with your mouth, but silently. Mark off each foot (in most cases, two syllables) and place a stress mark over each accented syllable. Remember: the meter is _not_ rigid; there will be variations.

7. Now have one member of the class play Macbeth, and another play Banquo. Let these two read the excerpt dramatically. Discuss the reading. Did "Macbeth" move smoothly from line 37 to line 38? (There's no punctuation after line 37.) Should emphasis vary in some places? (For example, line 34: metrically, the emphasis should be on the second syllable, "you." Actually, the emphasis is needed on the first syllable, "Stay.")

By now, you should be "swinging along" in iambic pentameter. Just for fun, take a few minutes and describe anything—perhaps your teacher's policy about homework. But describe it, orally, in iambic pentameter.

If you survive this challenge, you'll never again be awed by iambic pentameter!

FOR DISCUSSION

The lines quoted in Chapters 27, 28, and 29 make up only a third of Act I, Scene iii, yet they yield a tremendous amount of information.

8. Do you know Macbeth better now? What have you learned about him in these lines? _How_ did you learn all this?

9. What have you learned about Banquo in these lines? _How_ did you learn all this? Remember: characterization through dialogue—through one character's reactions to events and to other people.

10. How would you now describe the friendship between Macbeth and Banquo?

11. If Macbeth suddenly discovered that he had been named thane of Cawdor, how would he react?

30. A Dagger of the Mind?
A Soliloquy
from Act II, Scene i

An outstanding soliloquy ends Act II, Scene i, as Macbeth, alone, ponders the plans made by him and his wife—plans to murder King Duncan and thereby to become King of Scotland.

Imagine Macbeth on stage. He is alone, Where would he probably stand? (See page 35.) Remember: a soliloquy gives the *thoughts* of the speaker. What he says is heard by no character in the play, but only by the audience.

Read the soliloquy. Remember the unaccented/accented pattern of iambic pentameter.

Is this a dagger which I see before me,	1
The handle toward my hand? Come, let me clutch thee.	2
I have thee not, and yet I see thee still.	3
Art thou not, fatal vision, sensible	4
To feeling as to sight? or art thou but	5
A dagger of the mind, a false creation,	6
Proceeding from the heat-oppressed brain?	7
I see thee yet, in form as palpable	8
As this which now I draw.	9
Thou marshal'st me the way that I was going;	10
And such an instrument I was to use.	11
Mine eyes are made the fools o' the other senses,	12
Or else worth all the rest: I see thee still;	13
And on thy blade and dudgeon gouts of blood,	14
Which was not so before. There's no such thing:	15
It is the bloody business which informs	16
Thus to mine eyes. Now o'er the one half-world	17
Nature seems dead, and wicked dreams abuse	18
The curtain'd sleep; witchcraft celebrates	19
Pale Hecate's offerings; and wither'd murder,	20
Alarum'd by his sentinel, the wolf,	21
Whose howl's his watch, thus with his stealthy pace,	22
With Tarquin's ravishing strides, towards his design	23
Moves like a ghost. Thou sure and firm-set earth,	24
Hear not my steps, which way they walk, for fear	25
Thy very stones prate of my whereabout,	26
And take the present horror from the time,	27
Which now suits with it. Whiles I threat, he lives:	28
Words to the heat of deeds too cold breath gives.	29

[A bell rings.]

I go, and it is done: the bell invites me.	30
Hear it not, Duncan, for it is a knell	31
That summons thee to heaven, or to hell.	32

1. What is happening in lines 1–7? If you were making a movie and could use special effects, how would you enhance these lines?

_____

_____

_____

2. What action takes place in lines 8 and 9? Why does Macbeth draw a real dagger at this moment? (Consider the audience during this long speech. Could seeing the dagger add interest and suspense?)

_____

_____

_____

3. Paraphrase (put in your own words) lines 10 and 11. (''Marshal'st'' means ''conduct'' or ''lead.'')

_____

_____

4. Paraphrase lines 12 and 13.

_____

_____

5. What is the ''dudgeon''? Why does Macbeth see ''gouts of blood'' on the blade and dudgeon? (See pages 27 and 28.)

_____

_____

6. Macbeth changes mood suddenly in lines 15 to 17. What is he saying? How does he explain the bloody dagger to himself?

_____

_____

_____

7. Read lines 17–24. According to Macbeth, what happens at night? Name three things.

_____

_____

_____

8. Why does Shakespeare bring in references to Hecate and to Tarquin (see page 54)?

_____

_____

9. In lines 24–28, Macbeth "talks" to the earth. What does he say? Why should he expect nature to be influenced by the actions he has planned?

_____

_____

_____

_____

10. Explain the meaning of the last five words of line 28.

_____

_____

_____

_____

11. Explain the meaning of line 29. (Clue: think of "hot deeds" and "cold words." If you plan to do something daring and you stop to think of all the problems connected with it, what effect does this have on your project?)

_____

_____

12. Line 30. *What* is done?

_____

_____

13. Paraphrase lines 31 and 32.

_____

_____

14. Why do the last two lines rhyme? (See page 49.)

_____

_____

15. Is Macbeth going ahead with his plan? How do you know?

_____

16. Point out two allusions used in this soliloquy. (See page 53.)

_____

_____

17. Point out two examples of alliteration in this soliloquy. (See page 48.)

_____

_____

18. Have you learned anything new about Macbeth from this soliloquy? What?

_____

_____

_____

   Read the soliloquy again—this time, aloud. If you're shy, read it when you're alone, but tape record it (and, later, listen to it.) If you're a bit of a ham, read it dramatically for the entire class. Either way, the beauty of it, as well as the sense of it, should be coming through "loud and clear," just as it did to Elizabethan audiences nearly 400 years ago.

31. A Barren Scepter
A Soliloquy
from Act III, Scene i

   Another memorable soliloquy occurs in Act III, Scene i. Macbeth is now King of Scotland, but . . . What goes on in a murderer's mind, *after* the fact? Macbeth speaks.
   Read the soliloquy below. Remember the unaccented/accented pattern of iambic pentameter.

To be thus is nothing;	1
But to be safely thus: our fears in Banquo	2
Stick deep; and in his royalty of nature	3
Reigns that which would be fear'd: 'tis much he dares,	4
And, to that dauntless temper of his mind,	5
He hath a wisdom that doth guide his valor	6
To act in safety. There is none but he	7
Whose being I do fear: and under him	8
My Genius is rebuk'd, as it is said	9
Mark Antony's was by Caesar. He chid the sisters,	10
When first they put the name of king upon me,	11
And bade them speak to him; then prophet-like	12
They hail'd him father to a line of kings:	13
Upon my head they plac'd a fruitless crown	14
And put a barren scepter in my gripe,	15
Thence to be wrench'd with an unlineal hand,	16
No son of mine succeeding. If 't be so,	17
For Banquo's issue have I fil'd my mind;	18
For them the gracious Duncan have I murder'd;	19
Put rancors in the vessel of my peace	20

Only for them, and mine eternal jewel 21
Given to the common enemy of man, 22
To make them kings, the seed of Banquo kings! 23
Rather than so, come, fate, into the list, 24
And champion me to th' utterance! 25

1. (Lines 1–2) What is bothering Macbeth?

_____

_____

2. (Lines 2–8) We gain new insight into Banquo's character with these lines. What traits is Macbeth emphasizing?

_____

_____

3. (Lines 2–8) Find one example of alliteration. (See p. 48.)

_____

4. (Lines 8–10) Explain the allusion to Mark Antony and Caesar. Why, in your opinion, did Shakespeare use this allusion at this point? (See page 53.)

_____

_____

_____

5. (Lines 10–13) Which specific prophecies come sharply now to Macbeth's mind?

_____

_____

_____

6. (Lines 14–17) What has Macbeth come to realize about his winning of the crown? Is his attitude logical? Why, or why not?

_____

_____

_____

_____

7. (Lines 17–23) A second realization hits Macbeth. What is it?

_____

_____

8. (Line 22) Who is the ''common enemy of man''?

_____

9. (Line 21) Remembering your answer to 8, what does Macbeth mean by "mine eternal jewel"?

_____

10. (Lines 21–22) "Mine eternal jewel" is, of course, a metaphor. (See page 60.) In your opinion, why did Shakespeare use this metaphor here?

_____

_____

11. (Lines 17–23) A little time has passed since the murder of King Duncan. How does Macbeth feel about the deed now?

_____

_____

12. (Lines 24–25) Macbeth hurls these two lines into the air—a kind of defiance. What is his challenge? (See page 23 if you need help.)

_____

_____

Read the soliloquy again—this time, aloud. Are you beginning to feel the tight unity between meter and poetic techniques (e.g., alliteration) and content?

FOR DISCUSSION

13. You should know Macbeth a little better after you have read this soliloquy. Why? What have you learned about him?

14. What more have you learned about Banquo?

15. Put yourself in Macbeth's shoes. What is his next move? Considering his thoughts in this soliloquy, what *must* it be?

Notice how carefully Shakespeare used these few lines not only to provide background (which he did); not only to give you additional information about two of the main characters (which he did); but also to establish motivation for that which is to come. That, readers, is one of the reasons William Shakespeare's plays are still read and enjoyed today!

32. *Tomorrow, and Tomorrow, and Tomorrow*
A Soliloquy
from Act V, Scene v

Perhaps the most memorable soliloquy of all in *Macbeth* occurs in Act V, Scene v. Macbeth's world is falling apart. Malcolm and Macduff, with an army, are approaching Dunsinane. Lady Macbeth has just died, probably by her own hand. Macbeth still wears the crown; he still believes he can conquer his enemies. Yet triumph no longer tastes sweet upon his tongue. He muses.

Read the soliloquy. Remember the unaccented/accented pattern of iambic pentameter.

Tomorrow, and tomorrow, and tomorrow,	1
Creeps in this petty pace from day to day,	2
To the last syllable of recorded time;	3
And all our yesterdays have lighted fools	4
The way to dusty death. Out, out, brief candle!	5
Life's but a walking shadow, a poor player	6
That struts and frets his hour upon the stage	7
And then is heard no more: it is a tale	8
Told by an idiot, full of sound and fury,	9
Signifying nothing.	10

1. Read lines 1–3 slowly. How does the repetition of the word "tomorrow" reflect Macbeth's feeling about his present life?

_____

_____

2. (Line 2) An excellent example of alliteration is "petty pace." Read the line carefully. Now substitute a different alliterative phrase: "gaudy gait." Read the new line. Which alliterative phrase is better? Which best fits with Macbeth's mood? Support your answer.

_____

_____

_____

3. (Line 3) What does "the last syllable of recorded time" mean? What will be Macbeth's "last syllable of recorded time"? What will be *yours?*

_____

_____

_____

4. What do line 4 and the first half of line 5 mean?

_____

_____

_____

5. (Lines 4–5) Find an example of alliteration. Why is this alliterative phrase exactly right in this context?

_____

_____

6. (Line 5) "Out, out, brief candle!" is a brief sentence that interrupts and at the same time focuses Macbeth's thoughts. What is the "brief candle"? When does it go out? (Notice that "brief candle" is a metaphor. See page 60.)

_____

_____

7. (Lines 6–8) What is the metaphor that supports these two and a half lines?

_____

_____

8. (Lines 6–8) Considering the metaphor, explain briefly what Macbeth is thinking. (Look at all *parts* of the metaphor: e.g., "struts and frets.")

_____

_____

9. (Lines 6–8) Find an example of alliteration. Why is it exactly right in this context?

_____

_____

10. (Lines 8–10) These lines are based on a second metaphor. What is it?

_____

11. (Lines 8–10) Considering the metaphor, explain briefly what Macbeth is thinking.

_____

_____

12. (Line 10) What do the words "signifying nothing" mean?

_____

Read the soliloquy again, preferably aloud.

FOR DISCUSSION

13. What conclusions has Macbeth reached about life in general?

14. Have *you* ever felt the way Macbeth feels at this moment?

15. From this brief ten-line soliloquy have come many book titles.

> *The Sound and the Fury* (William Faulkner)
> *Told by an Idiot* (Rose Macaulay)
> *Brief Candle* (Aldous Huxley)
> *Walking Shadows* (E.W. White)
> *A Poor Player* (H. Child)

This Petty Pace (B. Pinkerton)
Tomorrow and Tomorrow (Philip Barry)
All Our Yesterdays (H.M. Tomlinson)
Dusty Death (C. Robbins)

In your opinion, why have so many authors sufficiently identified with this passage to select a phrase from it as the title of a book?

16. In one sentence, what is the meaning of these ten lines?

_____

_____

Take a few minutes now and memorize this brief soliloquy. Let the meter help you; let the alliteration help you; above all, let the *meaning* help you.

Once you have memorized it, you will forever have:

> A "feel" for iambic pentameter
> An understanding of Shakespeare's use of alliteration
> An insight into Macbeth's character—and end
> and
> A permanent reminder of Shakespeare's genius!

Best of all, perhaps, you will have a sort of talisman, a charm, that you can shout into the wind or mumble beneath the bedcover when *you* are feeling that life has passed you by. Try it. It will remind you that, when you reach for the stars, the stars may burn your fingers. It will remind you that the occasional doubt and dread you feel, you share with all humanity.

All this—from *Macbeth*.

FRANKLIN PIERCE COLLEGE LIBRARY

00101654